Finding Comfort After

Pet Loss:

A Guide for Grieving Pet

Owners

By

Nancy MacFarlane RVT

Dedication

I am dedicating this book to anyone who has deeply loved a pet and experienced the loss of their beloved pet. May you find the answers you are looking for that will lead you on a journey to comfort and peace.

To my friends and family who always encourage me to follow my heart.

To Reuben D'Souza – Thank you for being a cheerleader in my corner.

To Onnig Cavoukian – my famous photographer friend who gave me my most cherished possession – a portrait of my soul mate, my best friend Cairnbrae's Peaches n Cream, aka Miss Peaches.

Acknowledgment

There are many people I would like to thank, and it would be a long list, so instead, let me thank several groups that were key to making this book happen.

Many of my friends, teachers, and coworkers, with whom I have been fortunate enough to cross paths, have shaped the person I am today.

Now is my turn to give back to my profession and use my new knowledge to help others gain the insights that I have.

The Veterinary profession is like no other. We face all the same challenges that human medicine does, except our patients cannot speak, so we learn to read the body language and emotions of those we touch. All the pets I have cared for while working in veterinary clinics have taught me something.

End-of-life care is not something we have been taught much about in school, yet the impact it has on our daily lives is tremendous. And when you are new to the field, you have no idea how to deal with things at that moment. There are ways to cope with the emotions surrounding the end of life, dealing with grief, mourning the loss, and moving on afterward.

I would like to thank the University of Tennessee for allowing me to be the first Canadian RVT to enroll and complete the

Veterinary Human Support certificate program, where I learned so much about providing support to the veterinary teams and talking about the very things we do not talk about which leads to compassion fatigue and burnout.

Thank you to Pet Loss Partners for the creation of their course Pet Loss and Bereavement Specialist. I learned a lot in a short time about pet loss in general and how to be a compassionate listener for our grieving clients.

And, of course, many thanks to you, the reader.

To each and every one of you, I hope you find the answers you are looking for in this book. And if nothing else, let it be comfort for your soul to know you are not alone on this journey.

Sincerely,

Nancy

Contents

About the Author

Nancy & Trixie

Nancy MacFarlane is a Registered Veterinary Technician and a well-respected veterinary professional who has dedicated over 40 years to helping animals live their best life.

Nancy studied veterinary technology at St. Clair College in Windsor, Ontario, Canada, graduating in 1980. She later added certifications in Veterinary Social Work - Veterinary Human Support - at the University of Tennessee in October 2020 and Pet loss Bereavement Specialist Certification from Pet Loss Partners in 2023.

It was Nancy's childhood dream to become a veterinarian and work with animals. When she was in high school, she landed her first job working in a veterinary clinic as an animal care attendant. It was that job that determined her life path as a Veterinary Technician.

Nancy has owned and loved many pets of her own, including her favorite dogs – Jack Russell Terriers Peaches and Trixie, Siamese cat – Maddison, and her 2 oriental shorthairs she currently owns – Charlotte and Chester and Jack Russell terriers Tucker and Sunny.

Her experiences and fulfilling career have led her to write this book as a resource to help pet owners navigate end-of-life decisions, from choices to dealing with the loss and the grief that follows. Whether you own a dog, cat or any other type of pet this book is for you. What I have written here refers to dogs to share information. The process is the same regardless of the type of pet you have loved and lost.

I hope you find what you are looking for and please know that you are not alone in this journey.

Nancy MacFarlane RVT

I would like to share with you the following words from a friend of mine and Fellow RVT, Amanda Ellis, who has captured the very essence of a pet's life.

No one talks about the grief of watching your pet get old.

No one talks about how difficult it is to watch them slow down

No one tells you how much you'll long for those weekend hikes

No one talks about how heartbreaking it is to watch them struggle to get onto their favourite couch

No one tells you about the confusion in their eyes when they can no longer do certain things

No one talks about how, more often than not, they won't seem present

No one tells you that one day, they may just lose that spark in their eye

No one talks about how you'll miss the little quirks you use to scold them for

No one tells you about the joy you will get for those few seconds their personality comes back

No one talks about how you wish they could talk so they could tell you where it hurts

No one tells you how hard it is when you can't always be with them

No one talks about the grief of watching your best friend get old.

Here's to all the pet parents with senior best friends.

Just because no one talks about it doesn't mean you are alone

Permission to share: Amanda Ellis RVT

Chapter 1
The story of Peaches

Cairnbrae's Peaches and Cream

I am a firm believer that our pets chose us, not the other way around. They come into our lives when we need them the most, and the story of how I came to have an incredible relationship with Peaches is no different.

We had made the decision a few months earlier to add a Jack Russell Terrier to our family as our Doberman Chelsea was just over 9 years old, and I did not want to be dog less when her time came.

So the search began for a breeder that we could choose a puppy, and we found Gaye Redpath, a well-known longtime breeder here in Ontario, Canada, where we live. We met with her and her dogs, falling in love with these little terriers at first sight. We left a deposit on a future breeding for a puppy. Well, as the story goes, we were not able to get a puppy from Gaye's litter as I wanted a tan & white broken-coated female puppy, and she did not have one in the litter we chose when they were born. Here's where the story gets better. Her friend Shirley Buist, who also breeds quality Jack Russel terriers, just happened to have a litter of puppies with the same sire, and you guessed it; she had the exact puppy I was looking for. We fell in love with her instantly, and she came home with us that day.

Peaches, as she was named, became my best friend and little shadow. Our relationship was like no other. I swear this little dog could read my mind. Those of you who have had a similar attachment will understand that nothing can prepare you for the day this all disappears from your life. You experience a hurt like no other and no one else can relate to. It created an immense void that no other dog could fill or even come close to.

These types of deep relationships are very unique and not the norm when it comes to loving a pet. Each pet we have has a specific purpose in our lives, and that cannot be replaced with another pet, nor should it be. I have seen it before when owners try to replace the dog they just lost with the same breed, color, and sex. They even name it the same. I remember one client who came to our veterinary clinic who loved Shih Tzu's and was on Princess number 4 in our files.

As the years moved past us my relationship with Peaches only got deeper and deeper. While she loved everyone, especially our babysitter Trudy, who spoiled her rotten, it was me she was attached to the most. When our pets feel the same attachment as we do, it gives that person additional emotional connection and bonds. When the pet finally leaves us, it sends us into total despair, and all the emotions of grief come crashing down upon us all at once. We will talk about the emotional rollercoaster of feelings and grief, how to navigate them, and what to do when you are in this stage of grieving.

While we do not have a timeline for living with our pets, I was blessed to have had her in my life for 17.5 years. Think about that for a moment. That's over a decade and a half. There is a long list of memories that were made during that time, and as you take inventory of those memories you made with your pet, you will need them to help you cope with the ultimate loss.

You may be thinking; how can those memories help right now when I am hurting so much? I can tell you from experience that those very memories are exactly what you will draw upon to help you with the healing process.

I used to have a dog training school called Kamp K-9, teaching classes for 18 years in Grimsby, Ontario, where I lived. I met many pet owners and numerous puppies over the years.

It was there that I met Onnig Cavoukian and his puppy, Pasha. I very quickly realized the relationship they were embarking upon was very much like mine with Peaches. I could see that Pasha was in love with Onnig. I told him I could see it in Pasha's eyes; they looked at him just like my Peaches looked at me. A very deep right into your sole type of gaze.

As it turns out, I had no idea that Onnig is a famous photographer and has photographed Royalty and Dignitaries like Queen Elizabeth, her family, our Prime Pierre Minister Trudeau and his family and more.

When Pasha graduated from class, Onnig was kind enough to offer to photograph Peaches for me as a gift, which I accepted. At the time, it was a kind & thoughtful gesture, and the pictures turned out amazing. Years later, when Peaches passed away it was this kind gesture from Onnig that provided the most comfort in the healing process. In the beginning, it hurt to look at her picture because she was not here, and it just reminded me of the loss, making me sad. But over time, things changed, and the picture began to remind me of the great times we had together and how she changed my life for the better.

It's amazing how a simple, kind gesture has become one of my most treasured possessions, the very thing that helped me come full circle through the roller coaster of grief over the years to where I am today.

What Onnig did was immortalize Peaches for me so that I could always have her close, even if she was no longer here on this earth. I am forever grateful to Onnig Cavoukian and to call you my friend.

We will discuss ways to keep the memories of your cherished pet alive, too, so keep reading.

Chapter 2

Understanding Pet Loss

At the end of the day,
her best friend was always there with her, and that
is all that mattered.

Finding Comfort After Pet Loss

Pets are often called "a blessing with four paws" because of their unique ability to bring joy and comfort into our lives. Some people may say, "It's just a pet," implying that their impact is minimal compared to humans. However, this perspective overlooks the profound ways pets can influence our well-being.

A pet is more than just an animal; they are a loyal companion. They offer unwavering love and companionship without expecting anything in return. Their presence can transform a house into a home, filling it with warmth and laughter. When you come home after a long day, your pet greets you with an enthusiasm that never fades. This genuine joy can lift your spirits, no matter how tough your day has been.

Pets also have a mysterious ability to sense our emotions. When you feel sad or stressed, they often respond with gentle nudges or by simply sitting close to you, offering silent support. This intuitive empathy can be incredibly comforting, providing emotional support that is often more impactful than words.

Moreover, pets encourage us to lead healthier lifestyles. They need regular exercise, which means their owners also get more physical activity. Daily walks or playtime in the park become opportunities for both exercise and relaxation, promoting physical and mental health. This routine can help reduce stress, improve cardiovascular health, and enhance overall well-being.

The bond between a pet and its owner is built on trust and mutual respect. This relationship teaches us important values like responsibility, patience, and compassion. Caring for a pet requires time and effort, but the rewards are immeasurable. Watching a pet grow and thrive under your care fosters a sense of achievement and purpose.

Pets also play a significant role in social interactions. They are natural icebreakers, helping to initiate conversations with strangers during walks or at the park. This can be particularly beneficial for people who are shy or have difficulty making social connections. The shared interest in pets creates a common ground for interaction, leading to new friendships and a sense of community.

People often say that time will heal the pain of losing a pet and that animals don't have emotions. However, those who say this might not understand the depth of the bond between a person and their pet. My pet was a dog; she was the one who never left my side, providing constant companionship and unconditional love. In times of trouble, when others might have judged me or walked away, my dog stayed close, offering unwavering support.

Dogs have an incredible ability to sense our feelings. When I felt lonely or upset, my dog would come to me, providing comfort without needing to say a word. This silent understanding and presence can be more powerful than any spoken reassurance. It's hard to explain to those who haven't experienced it how much a dog can mean in such moments. They don't see that my dog's loyalty and affection were not just simple animal behavior but a deep, emotional connection.

People might not realize how dogs can show empathy. My dog always knew when I was feeling down and would act in ways that showed she cared, whether by resting her head on my lap or staying close by my side. This behavior showed a kind of emotional intelligence that many people underestimate in animals. Those who say animals don't have emotions have likely never experienced this kind of bond.

When others left or judged, my dog remained a constant in my life. She never cared about my flaws or mistakes. Her love was pure and without conditions. This kind of love can be rare among people who often let biases and judgments affect their relationships. My dog loved me for who I was, not for what I had achieved or failed at. This is a powerful kind of support that many people might not understand.

Losing such a companion is incredibly hard. Time might dull the pain, but the memory of that unconditional love and unwavering loyalty stays with you. It's not just about losing a pet; it's about losing a friend who was always there for you.

They don't know how frightened I was the night her moans and pacing woke me up. My dog, which always slept beside me, was in distress, and it terrified me. This moment highlighted just how much she meant to me and how integral she was to my life. Her presence was a constant source of comfort and joy, making every day brighter.

People might not understand the depth of the bond we share. My dog's habit of sleeping beside me wasn't just a routine; it was a source of security for both of us. Her rhythmic breathing and warmth brought me Peace, especially on restless nights. Waking up to her discomfort filled me with fear and helplessness as I desperately wanted to ease her pain.

Every day, my dog enriched my life in countless ways. Her playful antics and wagging tail were daily reminders of joy and love. Her boundless energy and excitement were infectious, lifting my spirits no matter what was happening in my life. Her simple presence turned ordinary moments into cherished memories.

From morning walks to evening cuddles, my dog was a constant source of happiness. Her playful nudges and eager greetings made me feel special and loved. Each wag of her tail and every joyful bark were expressions of pure affection, untainted by judgment or expectation. Her joy in simple things reminded me to appreciate the little moments in life.

People might not realize how much my dog's companionship meant to me. She was there in good times and bad, offering a kind of support that words often failed to provide. Her loyalty was unwavering, and her love was unconditional. She didn't care about my mistakes or failures; she loved me for who I was.

My dog's presence was a daily reminder of the beauty of simple, unspoken bonds. She taught me about patience, empathy, and unconditional love. Her companionship provided a sense of stability and comfort that was incredibly reassuring. Whether we were playing, walking, or simply sitting together, her presence was a source of joy and Peace. I paid close attention to every change because she mattered so much to me.

They don't know how often I talked to my dog, shared my thoughts, and confided in her. She was always there, a silent but attentive listener. I cried with her during tough times and laughed with her during moments of joy. Her presence was a constant source of emotional support, offering a level of understanding and empathy that was uniquely comforting.

She was the only one who really listened without judgment or interruption. Her quiet companionship provided a safe space for me to express my feelings freely. This kind of unconditional acceptance is rare, and it made our bond even stronger. My dog's ability to be there for me in these ways was a testament to her importance in my life.

They don't know how well I treated my dog. Every action I took was rooted in love and care. From ensuring she had the best food to make sure she was comfortable and happy, I did everything I could to provide her with a good life. Her happiness and health were always my top priorities.

People might not see the countless small acts of kindness and care that go into looking after a dog. They might not understand the emotional investment involved in nurturing such a deep bond. Each moment spent comforting her, noticing her changes, talking to her, and being there for her was significant. These were expressions of my love and dedication.

Chapter 3

The Roller Coaster of Emotions

My dog was the only one who could sense when I was ill, in pain, sad, or afraid. Her intuition about my feelings was remarkable. When I felt down, she would come close, offering silent comfort with her presence. This unspoken understanding between us was unique and deeply comforting.

People don't realize what it's like to see your old dog trying to come over and say hello. As she aged, her movements became slower, and every effort she made to greet me was filled with determination and love. Watching her struggle yet persist in showing affection highlighted her unwavering loyalty and the depth of our bond.

When things went wrong, my dog was always there. Her constant presence provided a sense of stability and reassurance. No matter how tough the situation, she never left my side. Her companionship during difficult times was a source of strength, helping me navigate challenges with a bit more ease.

Her ability to sense my emotions made her an exceptional companion. When I was sick or in pain, she would stay close, offering comfort without needing words. Her empathy was evident in her actions, whether it was resting her head on my lap or simply staying near me. This kind of support was irreplaceable, creating a bond that words can't fully capture.

Seeing her age was both heartwarming and heartbreaking. Her attempts to greet me, despite her physical limitations, were filled with love and dedication. These moments underscored the depth of our connection and the mutual affection we shared. Her perseverance in showing her love was a testament to the strong bond between us.

My dog was my best friend who loved me unconditionally. Throughout her life, she trusted me completely. Every moment we shared, from the joyful times to the challenging ones, was built on a foundation of mutual trust and love. She relied on me without hesitation, and that bond remained strong right up to her very last breath.

People don't realize the depth of this connection. My dog's unwavering trust in me was evident in everything she did. Whether we were playing, walking, or simply sitting together, her eyes always showed complete confidence in me. This trust was a testament to our strong relationship, one that was built on countless shared moments of care and affection.

I made a promise to give her the best life possible. From the moment she came into my life, I was determined to ensure her happiness and well-being.

When her time came to cross the Rainbow Bridge, it was one of the hardest moments of my life. The bond we shared made the farewell incredibly painful, but I knew I had kept my promise to give her the best life. In those final moments, her trust in me was still there, and I did everything I could to ensure her comfort and Peace.

The Rainbow Bridge is a concept often used to provide comfort to those grieving the loss of a beloved pet. According to this idea, when a pet dies, they cross a mythical bridge that connects Earth to a peaceful, beautiful meadow. In this serene place, pets are free from pain and suffering, running and playing joyfully.

The concept suggests that the pets remain in this idyllic place, waiting for their human companions to join them. When the pet owner's time comes, they cross the Rainbow Bridge together, never to be separated again. This idea is meant to offer solace by imagining a reunion with the pet in a blissful, eternal environment where love and companionship continue forever.

The imagery of the Rainbow Bridge has become widely accepted and cherished among pet owners. It provides a comforting narrative that helps cope with the emotional pain of losing a pet, emphasizing the enduring bond between humans and their animal companions.

I was there with her, stroking her fur and kissing her face. I whispered her name and told her, "I love you." In those final moments, I wanted her to feel my love and presence. Saying Goodbye was one of the hardest things I've ever had to do.

The ache in my heart is always there, a constant reminder of the void she left in my life. This emptiness is profound because she wasn't just any dog; she was my dog, Peaches. Our bond was unique and irreplaceable. The loss is a heavy burden, and the pain of her absence never truly fades.

Peaches brought immense joy and comfort into my life. Her loyalty, love, and companionship were unwavering. Every moment we spent together, from playful afternoons to quiet evenings, was filled with mutual affection and understanding. Her presence was a source of stability and happiness that can't be replaced.

Saying Goodbye to Peaches was incredibly painful, but it was important to me that she felt loved and comforted until the end. As I whispered her name and told her I loved her, I hoped she understood how much she meant to me. Her legacy lives on in my heart, and her memory will always be cherished.

Peaches, I love you. Run free and rest easy. Your spirit will always be with me, and the love we shared will never fade. Though the pain of losing you is immense, the joy you brought into my life was even greater. Thank you for being my loyal companion, my source of comfort, and my dear friend.

You'll meet me in the light

I know that you can't see me.
but trust me I'm right here.
Although I'm up in heaven.
my love for you stays near.

So often I see you crying.
many times you call my name.
I want so much to lick your face
and ease some of your pain.

I wish that I could make you see
that Heaven indeed is real.
If you could see me run and play
how much better you would feel.

But our loving God has promised me
that when the time is right.
you'll step out of the darkness and
meet me in the light.

Chapter 4
What is Grief?

Grief is a natural response to loss, but it's more than just feeling sad. It's a complex emotional journey that people go through when they experience a significant loss, such as the death of a loved one ,death of a pet, the end of a relationship, or a major life change like losing a job or facing a serious illness.

When someone experiences grief, it can affect them emotionally, physically, mentally, and spiritually. Emotionally, they might feel a wide range of emotions, such as sadness, anger, guilt, confusion, or even numbness. Physically, grief can manifest as fatigue, changes in appetite, sleep disturbances, aches and pains, or other physical symptoms. Mentally, it can affect concentration, memory, decision-making, and overall cognitive function. Spiritually, it can challenge a person's beliefs, values, and sense of meaning in life.

The process of grief is not linear; it doesn't follow a set timeline or predictable stages. Instead, it's more like a rollercoaster with ups and downs, twists and turns. People may move back and forth between different emotions and experiences as they navigate their grief journey. Some days might feel easier than others, while some moments might trigger intense waves of emotion.

It's important to recognize that grief is unique to each individual. There's no right or wrong way to grieve, and everyone's experience is valid. Factors such as personality, culture, beliefs, past experiences, and the nature of the loss can all influence how someone grieves.

One common framework for understanding the process of grief is the "stages of grief" model proposed by psychiatrist Elisabeth Kübler-Ross. According to this model, people may go through stages such as denial, anger, bargaining, depression, and acceptance. However, it's essential to remember that not everyone experiences these stages in the same way or in any particular order. Some people may skip certain stages altogether, while others may revisit them multiple times.

In addition to the emotional aspects, grief also involves practical tasks and adjustments. This might include making funeral arrangements, sorting through belongings, handling financial matters, or figuring out how to live life without the person or in this case the pet that was lost.

It's crucial for individuals experiencing grief to seek support from friends, family, or professionals if needed. Talking about their feelings, expressing their emotions, and receiving validation and understanding can be incredibly helpful in the grieving process. Counseling, support groups, and other resources are also available to provide additional assistance and guidance.

Ultimately, grief is a natural and necessary part of the human experience. While it can be incredibly painful and challenging, it also offers an opportunity for growth, healing, and finding meaning amidst loss. By acknowledging and honoring their grief, individuals can gradually find their way forward and learn to live with their loss in a way that feels meaningful to them.

What is Anticipatory Grief?

Anticipatory grief is the sadness and emotional distress that people feel when they know that a significant loss is imminent. It's like grieving before the actual loss happens. This type of grief commonly occurs when someone is facing the impending death of a loved one, including a pet.

When a pet is terminally ill or reaching the end of its life due to old age, pet owners often start to experience anticipatory grief. They may feel a mix of emotions, such as sadness, anxiety, guilt, and helplessness, as they anticipate the loss of their beloved animal companion.

One of the reasons anticipatory grief can be so intense is that pet owners start to mentally prepare themselves for life without their pets. They may imagine what it will be like to no longer have their furry friend by their side, to no longer hear their meows or feel their warm presence. This anticipation of loss can lead to a profound sense of sadness and emptiness.

Pet owners may also experience anticipatory grief as they witness their pet's decline in health. They may feel heartbroken to see their once-active and playful pet become weak, lethargic, or in pain. The anticipation of their pet's suffering can be emotionally overwhelming, and they may struggle with feelings of guilt or helplessness for not being able to alleviate their pet's pain.

Additionally, pet owners may start to anticipate the practical aspects of their pet's death, such as making end-of-life decisions, planning for euthanasia, or preparing for the inevitable grief that will follow. These anticipatory thoughts and emotions can be incredibly challenging to cope with, and pet owners may feel a profound sense of loss even before their pet has passed away.

Despite the emotional pain, anticipatory grief can also offer pet owners an opportunity to cherish the time they have left with their pets and to make the most of their remaining days together. They may choose to create special memories, spend quality time bonding, and express their love and gratitude for their furry companion.

It's essential for pet owners experiencing anticipatory grief to seek support from friends, family, or professionals who understand and validate their feelings. Talking about their emotions, expressing their concerns, and receiving empathy and support can help pet owners navigate this difficult time with greater resilience and strength.

What is Disenfranchised Grief?

Disenfranchised grief is a type of mourning that occurs when someone experiences a significant loss that is not openly acknowledged or socially supported. It's like grieving in silence, without the validation or recognition from others that their grief is legitimate and deserving of compassion.

This type of grief can stem from various situations. For example, it might occur when someone loses a relationship that was not officially recognized or approved by society, such as the death of a partner in a same-sex relationship in a community where it is not accepted. In this case, the surviving partner may feel unable to openly express their grief or receive support from others due to societal stigma or discrimination.

Disenfranchised grief can also arise in situations where the loss is considered less significant or worthy of mourning by others. For instance, the loss of a pet, a miscarriage, the death of an ex-spouse, or the loss of a distant relative may be downplayed or dismissed by others as not deserving of intense grief. As a result, individuals experiencing these losses may feel isolated, misunderstood, or invalidated in their grief.

One of the challenges of disenfranchised grief is that it can lead to feelings of loneliness, shame, or guilt for the person mourning the loss. They may internalize the message that their grief is not valid or acceptable, which can intensify their emotional pain and make it harder for them to seek support.

Moreover, without acknowledgment or validation from others, individuals experiencing disenfranchised grief may struggle to find outlets for their emotions or opportunities to memorialize their loss. They may feel pressure to suppress their feelings or to grieve in private, which can prolong their healing process and hinder their ability to cope with their loss effectively.

It's important to recognize that all forms of grief are valid and deserving of empathy and support, regardless of whether they are openly acknowledged or socially sanctioned. Everyone's experience of loss is unique, and no one should be made to feel ashamed or invalidated in their grief.

To address disenfranchised grief, it's crucial for individuals to seek out supportive communities, whether online or in person, where they can find understanding and acceptance. Counseling or therapy can also be helpful in providing a safe space for individuals to explore and process their feelings without fear of judgment.

Additionally, it's essential for society as a whole to become more aware and inclusive of the diverse experiences of grief. By fostering empathy, understanding, and validation for all forms of loss, we can create a more compassionate and supportive environment where everyone feels seen, heard, and valued in their grief journey.

Stages of Grief

a. shock and denial: Initially, when someone faces a significant loss, they may feel stunned or numb. It's like their mind struggles to grasp the reality of what has happened. They might find themselves saying things like, "This can't be true," or "It's just a bad dream." This stage serves as a protective mechanism, allowing individuals to gradually come to terms with the reality of their loss at their own pace.

b. pain and guilt: As the Shock wears off, the pain of the loss begins to sink in. People may experience intense emotional pain, sorrow, or regret. They might replay past events in their minds, wondering if they could have done something differently to prevent the loss or feeling guilty about things left unsaid or undone. This stage can be incredibly challenging as individuals confront the raw emotions associated with their loss.

c. Anger: Grief often brings forth feelings of anger. People may direct their anger towards various targets, including themselves, the person they lost, other people involved in the situation, or even a higher power or the universe itself. This anger can be a natural response to feeling helpless or unfairly treated by the circumstances of the loss. It's important for individuals to find healthy ways to express and manage their anger during this stage.

d. Depression and loneliness: As the reality of the loss sets in, people may sink into a state of sadness, emptiness, or despair. They may feel a profound sense of loneliness, even if surrounded by supportive loved ones. This stage is characterized by a deep longing for what has been lost and a struggle to find meaning or purpose in life without it. It's important for individuals to seek support and reach out for help if they find themselves overwhelmed by feelings of depression or hopelessness.

These stages of grief are not rigid or linear, and individuals may move back and forth between them or experience them in a different order. Additionally, not everyone will experience all of these stages, and some people may have unique ways of coping with their grief. The important thing to remember is that grief is a deeply personal and individual experience, and there is no right or wrong way to grieve.

e. Finding ways to cope: Coping with grief involves finding strategies and resources to help manage the intense emotions and challenges that come with loss. This might include seeking support from friends, family, or support groups, engaging in activities that bring comfort or distraction, practicing self-care and self-compassion, and seeking professional help if needed. Coping mechanisms can vary widely from person to person, and it's essential for individuals to find what works best for them.

f. Rebuilding life without the pet: After the initial shock and pain of the loss begin to ease, people may gradually start to adapt to life without their pet. This stage involves making adjustments and finding ways to fill the void left by the pet's absence. It might involve creating new routines, finding ways to honor the pet's memory, or opening up to the possibility of welcoming a new pet into their lives in the future. While rebuilding a life without a pet can be challenging, it also offers an opportunity for growth, resilience, and finding joy in new experiences.

g. Acceptance and hope: The final stage of the grieving process is often marked by acceptance and hope. This doesn't mean that the pain of the loss completely disappears or that the person forgets about their pet. Instead, it means coming to terms with the reality of loss and finding a sense of Peace and acceptance when moving forward with life. It's about recognizing that while the loss will always be a part of their story, it doesn't define their entire life or future happiness. This stage is also characterized by a renewed sense of hope and optimism for the future as individuals begin to look forward to new possibilities and experiences.

"I loved you for your whole life and I'll miss you for the rest of mine."

Chapter 5

When is The Right Time to Say Goodbye?

Studies have shown that losing a pet can be just as difficult as losing a close relative. Our pets become part of our family, a source of constant companionship and unconditional love. There isn't a perfect time to say Goodbye, and there is no easy answer, but there are ways to know when letting go might be the most compassionate choice for your beloved animal.

Think about your pet when they were at their healthiest and happiest. Perhaps your dog's tail wagged excitedly, or your cat's fur was sleek, and their eyes sparkled. Now, gently compare that image to how your pet is doing currently. Are they still enthusiastic about the activities they once loved? Does your dog or cat still enjoy walks, playtime, or cuddling?

Here's the thing: sometimes, our pets can't tell us exactly how they feel. They can't say, "Hey, my back hurts so much I can't play fetch anymore." But they will show us in their own way. Understanding these subtle signs is crucial for pet parents.

Listen to their little bodies: Their bodies are a window into their well-being, and changes in appetite, water intake, mobility, and sleep patterns can all be indicators of discomfort or underlying health issues.

Are they eating less? A healthy pet typically has a consistent appetite and enjoys their meals. Pay attention if your pet starts refusing food, eats significantly less than usual, or shows disinterest in their favorite treats. This can be a sign of pain, dental problems, nausea, or other health concerns. A single picky day might not be a cause for alarm, but a steady decline in appetite for several days warrants a visit to the veterinarian.

Are they drinking more or less? Just like with food, significant changes in water intake can be a red flag. Excessive thirst can be a symptom of diabetes, kidney disease, or other health problems. On the other hand, decreased water intake can indicate dehydration, which can be caused by illness, difficulty in water intake, or even dental issues that make drinking uncomfortable. Monitoring their water bowl and noting changes in their drinking habits can help you identify potential health problems early on.

Are they having trouble getting around? Mobility issues can develop gradually, especially with older pets. Observe their ability to perform everyday activities like jumping on furniture, climbing stairs, or going outside to use the bathroom. Difficulty navigating these tasks can indicate pain, joint problems, arthritis, or even neurological issues.

Are they sleeping more than usual? While some extra sleep is normal, especially for senior pets, a constantly lethargic pet might be a cause for concern. Pay attention to the quality of their sleep as well. Are they restless or uncomfortable? Do they seem deeply asleep but wake up disoriented? Changes in sleep patterns can be a sign of pain, illness, or even depression.

Look for changes in their mood: Their emotional state can also offer valuable clues about their well-being. A happy and engaged pet will typically show interest in their surroundings, interact with you playfully, and greet you with enthusiasm.

Do they seem withdrawn or disinterested in things they used to love? A previously playful pet who suddenly becomes withdrawn or aloof might be experiencing pain, anxiety, or depression. Pay attention to their energy levels and whether they seem to take pleasure in activities they once enjoyed, like chasing toys, going for walks, or cuddling on the couch.

Are they grumpy or irritable, even when you try to pet them? Changes in temperament can also be a sign of discomfort. A pet that snaps or growls when touched where it wasn't bothered before might be indicating pain in a specific area.

Do they seem confused or disoriented? Cognitive decline can occur in older pets, and disorientation or confusion can manifest in various ways. Are they wandering aimlessly around the house, seeming lost in familiar surroundings? Have they started having accidents in the house after previously being potty-trained? These changes in behavior can signal underlying health problems that require veterinary attention.

Trust your gut: As the one who knows your pet best, you have a unique ability to pick up on subtle changes in their behavior and personality.

By being attentive to these subtle changes in your pet's behavior and body language, you can become an advocate for their well-being. Early detection of potential health problems can lead to better treatment outcomes and improve your pet's quality of life. Don't hesitate to schedule an appointment even if you can't pinpoint a specific symptom. A thorough veterinary examination can help identify potential health problems early on when they are often easier to treat and manage.

Remember, quality of life is key: Medical advancements mean pets can live longer lives than ever before. But just because they can live longer doesn't mean they always should. If your pet is constantly in pain, despite medication, or if they can't do the things that make them happy anymore, it might be time to consider letting go.

In the next chapter we will discuss using a quality of life tool that will help you figure out your pets current state for quality of life which may help with making the tough decision to say good bye.

This doesn't mean giving up: Don't mistake considering euthanasia for giving up on your pet. Talk to your veterinarian about pain management options. Veterinary medicine has made great strides in pain management, and there might be medications, therapies, or even acupuncture that can make your pet more comfortable for a while longer. The goal is to ensure your pet enjoys their golden years as much as possible.

It's okay to grieve: Saying Goodbye to a pet is a huge loss. They become cherished members of the family, and their absence leaves a gaping hole in our hearts. Don't feel pressured to bottle up your emotions or pretend you're okay. Talk to friends and family who understand the unique bond between humans and pets, and allow yourself to grieve openly. Crying is a natural and healthy part of the grieving process. There are even pet bereavement groups available online and in some communities that can offer support and understanding from people who have walked a similar path. Remember, you're not alone in your grief.

Remember the good times: While the pain of loss is fresh, take time to celebrate the life of your furry friend. Look at pictures, reminisce about funny moments, and share stories with loved ones. Focus on the joy your pet brought you, the unconditional love they showered upon you, and the happy memories you created together. Creating a scrapbook or memory box filled with photos and keepsakes can be a comforting way to remember your pet and the special place they held in your life.

You gave them a great life: By making this difficult decision, you're showing your pet just how much you love them. Letting go isn't an act of abandonment; it's a final act of love and compassion. You're giving them the gift of Peace and freedom from pain. Remember, the decision isn't about what's easiest for you but about what's best for your pet. Choosing euthanasia allows them to escape suffering and ensures they spend their final moments surrounded by love and care.

There's no right or wrong answer here. The decision is yours, and it's never an easy one. There will be moments of doubt and second-guessing, and that's perfectly normal. But by following your heart, listening to your pet's subtle cues, and trusting your gut instinct, you can know you're doing what's best for your furry friend. No matter how difficult the decision may be, remember the love you shared and the wonderful life you gave your pet.

Chapter 6
Quality of Life Score Chart

Understanding the quality of life (QoL) of our pet animals is crucial for ensuring their well-being and making informed decisions about their care. To explore this topic comprehensively, let's delve into what a Quality of Life Score Chart entails, backed by studies and insights from reputable journals.

What is a Quality of Life Score Chart?

A Quality of Life Score Chart is a tool used by veterinarians and pet owners to assess various aspects of an animal's well-being. It helps gauge how comfortable and content an animal is in its current state of health and environment. The chart typically consists of several categories or parameters, each with a set of criteria that are scored to provide an overall assessment.

Parameters in a Quality of Life Score Chart

Physical Comfort: This includes factors such as pain level, mobility, and ability to perform daily activities without difficulty. Studies have shown that animals experiencing pain or discomfort may exhibit changes in behavior, such as decreased activity or increased aggression.

Example: A study published in the Journal of Veterinary Behavior found that dogs with osteoarthritis showed improved QoL scores when pain management strategies were implemented, leading to better mobility and overall comfort.

Behavioral State: This parameter assesses the animal's behavior and interaction with its environment. Signs of stress, anxiety, or depression can indicate a reduced quality of life. Observing changes in eating habits, social interaction, and playfulness are crucial here.

Example: Research highlighted in the Journal of Applied Animal Welfare Science demonstrated that environmental enrichment, such as providing stimulating toys or interaction, can positively impact the behavioral state of shelter cats, leading to higher QoL scores.

Psychological Well-being: This category considers the mental health and emotional state of the animal. Factors like stress levels, fear, and the presence of any psychological disorders are evaluated. Pets experiencing psychological distress may exhibit withdrawn behavior or aggression.

Example: A study in the journal Animals examined the effects of housing conditions on the psychological well-being of laboratory animals, emphasizing the importance of social housing and enrichment activities in maintaining positive QoL scores.

Functionality: This parameter assesses the animal's ability to perform essential functions such as eating, drinking, grooming, and elimination. Any impairments or difficulties in these activities can significantly impact their QoL.

Example: Research published in Veterinary Record explored the impact of chronic conditions such as diabetes on cats' functionality and QoL, highlighting the importance of regular monitoring and management to maintain optimal health.

Environmental Adaptation: This considers how well the animal adapts to its living conditions, including factors like temperature, cleanliness, and access to resources. Poor environmental conditions can lead to stress and discomfort.

Example: Studies in the Journal of Veterinary Behavior have shown that ensuring a suitable environment, including proper housing and hygiene, plays a vital role in enhancing the QoL of pet rabbits and minimizing stress-related behaviors.

Importance of Using a Quality of Life Score Chart

Using a QoL score chart provides several benefits for both pet owners and veterinarians:

Early Detection of Issues: Regular assessments can help detect health or behavioral issues early, allowing prompt intervention and treatment.

Informed Decision Making: It assists in making informed decisions about treatment options, palliative care, or end-of-life decisions based on the pet's overall well-being.

Monitoring Progress: QoL assessments over time help monitor the effectiveness of treatments or changes in management practices.

Enhancing Communication: It facilitates communication between pet owners and veterinary professionals, ensuring that everyone involved understands the pet's needs and preferences.

Studies Supporting the Use of Quality of Life Score Charts

Numerous studies have validated the effectiveness of QoL score charts in assessing and improving the well-being of pets:

Research published in the Journal of the American Veterinary Medical Association demonstrated that using QoL assessments in elderly dogs with chronic illnesses helped in tailoring treatment plans to maintain comfort and functionality.

A study in the Journal of Veterinary Internal Medicine evaluated the application of QoL score charts in cats with chronic kidney disease, showing that monitoring QoL scores correlated with improved management of clinical signs and overall patient care.

Findings in the Journal of Feline Medicine and Surgery highlighted the utility of QoL score charts in evaluating pain management strategies in cats recovering from surgery, emphasizing the importance of multimodal approaches to enhance recovery and well-being.

Practical Application of Quality of Life Score Charts

Implementing QoL score charts involves systematic observation and documentation. Here's how it can be practically applied:

Initial Assessment: Conduct a comprehensive evaluation of the pet's current health status and behavior. Record baseline scores for each parameter in the QoL chart.

Regular Monitoring: Schedule periodic assessments to track changes in the pet's condition over time. Note any improvements or declines in QoL scores and adjust care accordingly.

Consultation with Professionals: Discuss QoL scores with your veterinarian or animal behaviorist to gain insights into potential interventions or adjustments to improve the pet's well-being.

Pet Owner Education: Educate pet owners about the importance of QoL assessments and how to recognize signs of discomfort or distress in their pets. Encourage proactive management and early intervention.

Challenges and Considerations

While QoL score charts are valuable tools, they come with certain challenges and considerations:

Subjectivity: Assessments may be subjective, influenced by individual perceptions or biases. Training and standardized protocols can help minimize variability.

Multifactorial Nature: QoL is influenced by multiple factors, including individual health, environmental conditions, and social interactions. A comprehensive evaluation is essential.

Ethical Considerations: Decisions based on QoL assessments, especially regarding end-of-life care, require careful ethical deliberation and respect for animal welfare.

Implementing quality of life (QoL) assessments for assessing a pet's well-being involves a structured approach to systematically evaluate various aspects of its health, behavior, and environment. Here's a step-by-step guide on how to implement QoL assessments effectively:

Step 1: Understand the Components of QoL Assessment

Before starting the assessment, familiarize yourself with the key components typically included in QoL evaluations:

Physical Comfort: Assess pain levels, mobility, and any physical limitations.

Behavioral State: Evaluate changes in behavior, social interaction, and emotional responses.

Psychological Well-being: Consider stress levels, anxiety, and signs of depression.

Functionality: Observe the ability to perform essential activities such as eating, drinking, and grooming.

Environmental Adaptation: Review the living conditions and how well they meet the pet's needs.

Step 2: Choose a QoL Assessment Tool or Chart

Select a QoL assessment tool or chart that aligns with the specific needs and characteristics of your pet. There are various resources available, including:

Veterinary-Developed Tools: Many veterinarians have specific QoL assessment charts tailored for different species or conditions.

Research-Based Tools: Tools validated through scientific studies provide reliability and consistency in assessment.

Ensure the chosen tool includes clear guidelines and scoring criteria for each parameter to maintain objectivity and consistency.

Step 3: Establish Baseline Scores and Parameters

Before implementing regular assessments, establish baseline scores for each parameter by conducting an initial evaluation of your pet's current state. This baseline will serve as a reference point for tracking changes over time.

Parameters may include:

Physical: Pain level (e.g., using pain scales), mobility (e.g., ability to walk or climb stairs), and overall physical condition.

Behavioral: Changes in activity levels, interactions with family members or other pets, and responses to stimuli.

Psychological: Signs of stress or anxiety, enjoyment of usual activities, and responsiveness to environmental changes.

Functional: Ability to eat, drink, eliminate waste, groom, and maintain overall self-care.

Environmental: Evaluation of living conditions, including comfort, cleanliness, and access to necessary resources (food, water, shelter).

Step 4: Implement Regular Monitoring and Assessment

Schedule regular QoL assessments to monitor your pet's well-being consistently. The frequency of assessments may vary based on factors such as the pet's age, health status, and any ongoing medical conditions. For example:

Daily Observations: Integrate quick daily assessments into your routine to observe changes in behavior, appetite, and interactions.

Weekly or Bi-weekly Assessments: Conduct more comprehensive assessments on a regular basis to track trends and identify potential concerns early.

Step 5: Document and Track Changes

Document each assessment session, recording scores for each parameter and any relevant observations or notes. Tracking changes over time allows you to identify patterns or deviations from baseline scores.

Use of Charts or Spreadsheets: Maintain organized records using QoL assessment charts, spreadsheets, or digital tools designed for tracking pet health and well-being.

Visual Representation: Consider using graphs or visual representations to visualize trends and changes in QoL scores over weeks or months.

Step 6: Consult with Veterinary Professionals

Discuss QoL assessment findings with your veterinarian during regular check-ups or as needed. Veterinary input can provide additional insights into interpreting scores, identifying underlying health issues, and recommending appropriate interventions or adjustments to care.

Step 7: Adjust Care Plans Based on QoL Assessments

Based on assessment results and veterinary recommendations, adjust your pet's care plan as necessary to enhance their QoL:

Medical Management: Implement pain management strategies, adjust medications, or incorporate therapies to alleviate discomfort.

Environmental Modifications: Enhance living conditions by providing enrichment activities, improving accessibility, or adjusting the environment to reduce stress.

Behavioral Interventions: Address behavioral changes through training, socialization, or behavior modification techniques.

Step 8: Consider End-of-Life Care and Decisions

QoL assessments also play a crucial role in end-of-life care decisions. Continuously evaluate your pet's QoL scores to determine when palliative care or humane euthanasia may be appropriate, ensuring their comfort and dignity.

Step 9: Educate and Involve Family Members or Caregivers

Ensure all family members or caregivers involved in the pet's daily care are familiar with QoL assessments and understand their importance. Encourage open communication and collaboration in monitoring and improving your pet's well-being.

Step 10: Continuous Improvement and Adaptation

Regularly review and refine your QoL assessment process based on feedback, new research, or changes in your pet's health status. Continuously seek opportunities to enhance their overall quality of life through proactive management and attentive care.

Knowing your dog's quality of life is essential for ensuring their happiness and well-being. This chapter will explore two methods for tracking your dog's quality of life: the HHHHHMM Scale and the Calendar Method.

The HHHHHMM Quality of Life Scale

Developed by Dr. Alice Villalobos, the HHHHHMM Scale provides a structured way to assess your dog's well-being across seven key areas:

Hurt: Does your dog seem in pain? (0 = constant pain, 10 = pain-free)

Hunger: Is your dog eating and drinking normally? (0 = no interest in food or water, 10 = eager to eat and drink)

Hydration: Does your dog seem well-hydrated? (0 = dehydrated, 10 = well-hydrated)

Hygiene: Is your dog able to keep themself clean? (0 = difficulty eliminating or maintaining cleanliness, 10 = able to eliminate and groom themself)

Happiness: Does your dog seem happy and content? (0 = no enjoyment in life, 10 = joyful and engaged)

Mobility: Can your dog move around comfortably? (0 = unable to move, 10 = full mobility)

More good days than bad: Does your dog have more good days than bad? (0 = mostly bad days, 10 = mostly good days)

Using the HHHHHMM Scale:

Score each category on a scale of 1 to 10. Consider your dog's usual behavior and any recent changes.

Add the scores together. A score of 63 or higher generally indicates a good quality of life. Lower scores may suggest a decline in well-being and warrant a discussion with your veterinarian.

Here's a sample score sheet you can copy and use:

Category	Description	Score (1-10)
Hurt	Pain level	
Hunger	Eating and drinking habits	
Hydration	Hydration status	
Hygiene	Ability to maintain cleanliness	
Happiness	Overall happiness and contentment	
Mobility	Ease of movement	
More good days than bad	The ratio of good days to bad days	
Total Score		

Remember: This scale is a guideline. Discuss any concerns you have with your veterinarian.

What is Considered "Quality of Life" for a Dog or cat?

Quality of life means different things to different people. At its most basic, this term refers to a dog's daily lifestyle, whether their basic needs are met, and how they are feeling. A good quality of life for a dog may include:

- Eating and drinking normal amounts (and looking forward to food and treats)

- Being able to play with toys, family members, or other dogs

- Enjoying activities like walks, hikes, or swimming

- Resting comfortably and being able to sleep (without excessive sleeping)

- Enjoying time spent with family members

- Being able to hold urine and feces until getting outside

- Having tolerable pain levels (or ideally no pain)

- Being free of fear or confusion

- Finding enjoyment in favorite activities

Regardless of which activities matter most to you and your dog, the general concept is the same: every dog deserves to be as happy, healthy, and comfortable as possible. This is true even—or perhaps especially—in times of illness and during a dog's senior years.

Calendar Method

A simple and useful way to get a snapshot of your dog's quality of life is to use a calendar. At the end of each day, decide if it was a "good day" or a "bad day" and write it down on the calendar.

Using one color for "good" and another for "bad" can provide a visual representation of the days.

If you count up the marks and notice that bad days are becoming more frequent than good ones, it might indicate that your dog's quality of life is declining.

Using A Quality Of Life Scale For Dogs

A quality of life scale for dogs can be a helpful way to objectively assess your dog's comfort, happiness, and overall well-being. Integrative veterinarian Dr. Julie Buzby explains the concept of quality of life, discusses ways to assess it (including sharing her favorite quality of life scales for dogs), and explains what to do when you see your dog's quality of life begin to decline.

Dogs play such an enormous role in our lives—as best friends, confidants, and family members. No matter what, we know they love us unconditionally.

However, the sad reality is that we often outlive our beloved dogs. As our dear companions begin to fade away, their quality of life may weigh heavily on our minds. We may watch and worry—questioning whether our beloved companions are still enjoying life.

One way to help answer that question is by using a quality-of-life scale for dogs. It can provide an objective way for you to evaluate your senior dog's quality of life and allow you to pick up on small changes in your dog that otherwise may go unnoticed. To understand the quality of life scale, let's start by defining "quality of life."

What is considered "quality of life" for a dog?

Quality of life means different things to different people. At its most basic, this term refers to a dog's daily lifestyle, whether his or her basic needs are met, and how he or she is feeling. A good quality life for a dog may mean:

- Eating and drinking normal amounts (and looking forward to food and treats)

- Being able to play with toys, family members, or other dogs

- Enjoying taking walks, hikes, swimming, etc.

- Resting comfortably and being able to sleep (but not sleeping excessively)

- Enjoying spending time with family members

- Being able to hold urine and feces until getting outside

- Having tolerable pain levels (or ideally no pain)

- Being free of fear or confusion

- Finding enjoyment in favorite activities

Regardless of which activities matter most to you and your dog, the general concept is the same. Every dog deserves to be as happy, healthy, and comfortable as possible. This is the case even— or perhaps especially—in times of illness and during a dog's senior years.

Why assess a dog's quality of life?

It can be natural to think more about quality of life when your dog has been diagnosed with a terminal disease or is struggling with the effects of aging. But these aren't the only reasons to make a conscious effort to think about your dog's current well-being. You may also want to consider quality of life when your dog is dealing with these situations:

Chronic medical conditions

Kidney failure in dogs, liver disease in dogs, Cushing's disease in dogs, seizures in dogs, osteoarthritis in dogs, dental disease in dogs, and other chronic diseases can take a toll on your dog over time.

Lifelong medications

Sometimes, side effects or the need to try to convince your dog to take pills day in and day out can become overwhelming.

Need for certain interventions.

Some dogs may need specialized care to meet their daily needs. For example, dogs who can't or won't eat on their own might need a feeding tube. While this is usually fairly non-invasive, it may impact the quality of life for dogs who need tubes constantly replaced or repaired.

As another example, a paralyzed dog may need help moving from place to place or expressing his or her bladder. This can alter the quality of life as well, especially if the dog previously enjoyed sleeping on the furniture, romping in the yard, or following someone from room to room.

Changes in hearing or sight

Many dogs who are blind and deaf adjust quite well to their condition. However, even if you do your best to communicate with your deaf dog or help your blind dog, these changes can be difficult for some dogs and may negatively impact their quality of life.

Cancer treatments

Thankfully, radiation and chemotherapy do not typically affect dogs as severely as they do humans. However, it is still important to be mindful of your pet's quality of life—both as a result of the treatments and due to the cancer itself. Cancer can affect a dog's energy, appetite, sleep schedule, and pain level.

Behavior changes

Canine cognitive dysfunction and the resulting signs of dementia in dogs can greatly impact your senior dog's personality and confidence. Also, dogs who have severe phobias or separation anxiety may be in a great deal of mental pain, even if they are physically well.

This list is good starting point, but it isn't comprehensive. When in doubt, talk to your veterinarian to see if he or she thinks you should be assessing your dog's quality of life on a regular basis.

How do you use a quality-of-life scale for dogs?

If you determine that you need to assess your dog's quality of life, a quality-of-life calculator or scale can be a helpful tool. Most are very user-friendly. Typically, they include a list of questions about your dog's daily life with either a rating scale or yes/no check boxes.

6 tips for using quality of life scales for dogs

Here are six tips that can help you get the most benefit out of your dog's quality of life assessment tool:

1. Know the benefits of using the same scale vs. mixing it up

Most of the time, once you find the quality of life scale that is right for you and your dog, it is best to stick with it. Using the same scale repeatedly gives you a baseline and a way to accurately compare results. Also, it means you will become familiar with the criteria. This allows you to unofficially evaluate your dog's quality of life during your day-to-day interactions.

As a caveat to this, there are times when it can be beneficial to alternate quality-of-life scales or use multiple ones. That approach can help you get a fresh look at your pet's quality of life. It may also help you see things that your original scale overlooked.

2. Work through the scale regularly.

Every scenario is different for every family, but I usually recommend working through the scale at least once a month initially. As your dog approaches the time when you might need to consider euthanasia, it can be beneficial to use the scale more often—perhaps every week or every day.

3. Evaluate a good day and a bad day to create a baseline.

In the beginning, it is helpful to use the scale on at least one "good day" and one "bad day." This helps you know what a "good day" looks like for your dog. It can also be a helpful reminder of the things your dog is still enjoying in life and what is really important to him or her.

On the flip side, having a baseline for "bad days" is also important. That way, you have an idea of what it looks like when your dog starts declining.

4. Pick a time (or times) of day to complete the evaluation.

For accuracy, evaluate your dog's quality of life at the same time of day. Sometimes, a dog's quality of life can vary throughout the day, which may skew the results. For example, if you assess your dog during his or her best time of day and then a week later evaluate it during his or her worst time of day, your results will not be as accurate.

There are also times when it can be helpful to use the quality of life assessment scale several times in the same day—perhaps in the morning and again in the evening or at night. This gives you an understanding of how your dog's quality of life may fluctuate throughout the day.

5. Involve your family and close friends in assessing your dog.

Are you unsure of how your dog is feeling? Concerned you might be missing clues as you observe your dog? You may want to consider asking a close family member or friend to answer a quality of life quiz for your dog. Also, a close friend may provide a more objective opinion.

Keep in mind that it is important to ask someone who knows your dog very well so they can answer the questions.

6. Enlist the help of your veterinarian.

Any time you are unsure of your answers or want help working through a quality-of-life checklist for your dog, remember that your veterinarian is there to support you. Thinking about quality of life and contemplating when you may need to say goodbye is one of the most difficult decisions you may make on your dog's behalf. Your veterinarian can be a compassionate and knowledgeable resource for you and your dog during this difficult time.

How do I find a good quality-of-life scale for dogs?

To find a good quality of life scale, don't hesitate to reach out to your veterinarian. Not only is your veterinary team a great resource, but some vets have a particular scale they recommend. Also, you may find a scale on your vet's own website or social media. If you prefer a hard copy, you can give your vet's office a call and ask to pick one up.

There are many quality-of-life quizzes online. Dog hospice, in-home euthanasia services, and veterinary school websites are all great places to find downloadable quality-of-life scales.

Additionally, you can use one of the scales I recommend:

HHHHHMM Quality of Life Scale

The HHHHHMM Quality of Life Scale (created by Alice Villalobos, DVM, DPNAP) is one of the most common scales. The five H's stand for Hurt, Hunger, Hydration, Hygiene, and Happiness. The two M's stand for Mobility and More good days than bad. Each of these categories has a question that you score on a scale of 1 to 10. The total scale will help you determine if your dog's quality of life is potentially declining.

OSU Quality of Life Scale

I also really like the Quality of Life Scale created by The Ohio State University Veterinary Medical Center. It is similar to the HHHHHMM scale but breaks those 7 broader categories into 25 more specific criteria that you rate individually on a scale of 1 to 5.

Both of these resources provide a dog quality of life scale pdf that you can easily print off and keep for your records. This allows you to look back at your answers from the previous weeks or months and compare them to your dog's current score.

Calendar method

A simple and useful way to get a snapshot of your dog's quality of life is to use a calendar. At the end of each day, decide if it was a "good day" or a "bad day" and write it down on the calendar.

Using one color for "good" and another for "bad" can give you a nice visual representation of the days.

If you count up the marks and the bad days are becoming more frequent than the good, your dog's quality of life might be declining.

DIY Quality of Life Scale

If you do not want to use one of the scales listed above, you also can create a basic scale for yourself. The easiest way to do this is to write down a list of activities that your dog loves to do. If you begin noticing that you start answering "no" when you ask yourself if your dog likes to do those same things, then it is possible that your dog's quality of life is declining.

Finally, you may use the quality of life assessment below…

Dog Quality of Life ASSESSMENT — Dr. Buzby's

DATE:	YES	NO
Has your dog lost his or her appetite?	○	◉
Is your dog drinking excessively?	○	◉
Does your dog spend more time sleeping during the day than normal?	○	◉
Is your dog restless at night?	○	◉
Has your dog lost interest in going on walks?	○	◉
Has your dog stopped enjoying the things they love?	○	◉
Has your dog become less engaged in family activities?	○	◉
Does your dog choose to spend less time with you?	○	◉
Has your dog stopped greeting you at the door?	○	◉
Has your dog's behavior changed toward other pets?	○	◉
Does your dog get snippy or upset when you try to help them?	○	◉
Does your dog limp, whine, or show other signs of pain?	○	◉
Does your dog pant more than usual?	○	◉
Does your dog struggle to get up and walk without your help?	○	◉
Do you become frustrated or exhausted from caring for your dog?	○	◉
Is your own sleep negatively affected by your dog's needs?	○	◉

For other articles and resources on caring for your senior dog, visit ToeGrips.com.

© Julie Buzby, DVM, Dr. Buzby's Innovations, LLC. All Rights Reserved.

How does caretaker fatigue factor into the quality of life evaluations?

One of the most important questions on the quality of life assessment above is this one: "Do you become frustrated or exhausted caring for your dog? This question is an important (but difficult) one to ask yourself. Caretaker fatigue is real, and it is relevant to a quality-of-life discussion. You need to be able to recognize when you start becoming impatient or resentful toward your dog.

No matter how much we love our dogs, caring for them during their senior years or after a terminal diagnosis is hard. This can be especially true in cases where dogs are having accidents or are sick regularly. It also can happen when dogs need assistance moving around and rely on your help for simple tasks or when cognitive decline has changed their personality and behavior.

I know you love your dog and would do anything to help him or her. But I want you to know that it is okay and normal to become overwhelmed sometimes. If the challenges of caring for your dog are affecting your bond, talk with your veterinarian about ways to help you and help your dog.

What if you realize your dog's quality of life is declining?

You should also talk to your veterinarian when, based on the quality of life scale results, you suspect your dog's quality of life is declining. Your vet can help you interpret your dog's quality of life questionnaire and also assess your dog. Usually this involves looking at how your dog is doing physically and asking you some questions regarding your dog's behavior at home. The questions may be similar to those on the quality of life assessments.

With this information, your vet may make recommendations regarding how to proceed. Sometimes, there are ways to improve a dog's quality of life again once it starts to decline. Depending on the situation, these recommendations could include:

- Adding in pain medications such as gabapentin for dogs, amantadine for dogs, or tramadol for dogs

- Trying out dog nail grips or a Rx joint diet and joint supplement to improve your dog's mobility and comfort

- Changing your routines or modifying your at-home environment

- Trying a new medication or therapy for a chronic disease

- Giving appetite stimulants to dogs

- Other measures specific to your dog's situation

Unfortunately, there may come a time when you've exhausted all the options. In this situation, you may have to start talking about preparing for your dog's end-of-life decision or natural passing.

Saying goodbye

The hardest part of being blessed with a dog is the time when you have to say goodbye. No matter how long you have had with your dog, it is never going to be long enough. Many people express that losing a dog is harder than losing a friend. This is because dogs spend every day with us and become our best friends. Your dog is there for you no matter what.

If you are facing the difficult decision between dog hospice care or euthanasia, know that it is okay to not be sure how to proceed and to have a lot of questions. This is a very difficult time for you and your dog. Rely on family, friends, and your veterinarian (or a veterinarian who specializes in end-of-life care) to help you and your dog through this time.

You may also benefit from these articles:

- In-Home Dog Euthanasia: Heartfelt Answers to 12 FAQs [1]

- Dog Euthanasia: Knowing When to Say Goodbye [2]

- How Will You Know When It's Time to Euthanize Your Dog? 5 Caring, Heartfelt Messages [3]

- Grieving the Loss of a Dog After Euthanasia (& Finding Peace) [4]

- Dementia in Dogs: When to Euthanize Your Beloved Senior Dog [5]

Thinking about your dog's quality of life is good but hard

As you consider your dog's final days or months, a quality-of-life scale may give you clarity and direction. You know where your dog was. And you know where he or she is now. But I know it can be heartbreaking at the same time. Sometimes, seeing those checks or adding up the score may make your sweet dog's struggles all the more real.

Know that you are not alone in this. You have friends, family, and your veterinarian in your corner (and your dog's corner). They are here to help you…be that by filling out a quality-of-life scale for your dog, offering solutions, or being a listening ear and a shoulder to cry on.

Dementia in Dogs is another topic, as we do see this a lot more now with pets living longer, and this can be really challenging for owners.

Dementia In Dogs: When To say good bye to Your Beloved Senior Dog

If your grey-muzzled companion is in the end-stages of dementia in dogs, when to euthanize him or her may be a question that weighs heavily on your mind. To help give you some measure of peace and clarity, integrative veterinarian Dr. Julie Buzby invites Dr. Dawnetta Woodruff to the blog. As a veterinarian who specializes in end-of-life care, Dr. Woodruff is the perfect person to address this difficult decision with compassion and understanding.

Maybe you have a senior dog who is "just not himself" or "just not herself" lately. He or she paces the house, seems confused, pants a lot, barks at normal noises, and may even look at you as if you are a stranger. You may wonder what could possibly be wrong and how do you manage it?

There are a variety of conditions that could be the culprit. However, the most likely explanation is that your dog might be dealing with dementia, a condition that affects 68% of dogs by 16 years of age. While it can't be cured, there are some things you can do to help your dog continue to have a good quality of life. However, eventually, the time may come when you need to consider when to euthanize a dog who has dementia.

What is dementia in dogs?

Very few diseases are as frustrating and difficult to manage as canine dementia, which is also called canine cognitive dysfunction (CCD). When examined microscopically, the brain of a dog with dementia looks identical to the brain of a human with Alzheimer's disease. And like Alzheimer's patients, dogs with CCD suffer a decline in their cognitive function. Many advances are being made in treating both diseases, but there is currently no cure.

The earlier the veterinarian and dog owner start treatment, the better the dog will respond. However, in order to start treatments early, a dog must have an early diagnosis. There is no specific blood test or other lab work that can give you an official "yes or no." Instead, your veterinarian will diagnose CCD based on the symptoms your dog is showing.

Signs of dementia

It is important to consult with your vet if you think your dog may be starting to show any of these signs of dementia:

Disorientation

- Pacing

- Appearing lost

- Staring into space

- Acting confused

- Wandering room to room

- Getting "stuck" in a corner

Interaction changes

- No interest in seeing family

- Doesn't play with other pets in the home anymore

- Acting very aloof or very clingy

- New aggression toward family members or other pets

Sleep issues

- Sleeping more or less than normal

- Restless sleep

- Pacing at night

- Days and nights mixed up

- Senior dog anxiety at night

House Soiling

- Finding urine or feces in the home when your dog used to be fully housetrained

- Urinating or defecating in front of the owner inside

Altered Activity

- No longer interested in playing, taking walks, or being groomed

- Doesn't recognize learned commands

For a more in-depth look at how these signs are present, please read my article that specifically covers the signs of dementia in dogs.

Also, to help guide a conversation with your dog's veterinarian, you can print off a canine cognitive dysfunction checklist and take it with you to your dog's next vet visit.

How can you help a dog with dementia?

If your veterinarian diagnoses your dog with dementia, there are many things you can do to hopefully slow the progression of the disease and reduce the symptoms. Keeping the routine as predictable as possible can be very helpful for your dog. A regular feeding time, a regular sleep schedule, and a predictable time for play can be stable anchors within your dog's confusing day.

Rotating favorite toys in and out of the dog's toy box, adding puzzle toys, and spending extra time going on walks (or stroller rides) for mental stimulation can help your dog feel more like himself or herself.

Interestingly, a study from the University of Washington titled Evaluation of Cognitive Function in the Dog Aging Project: Associations with Baseline Canine Characteristics indicated that dogs who were not active were 6.47 times more likely to develop CCD than dogs who were very active. So regular activity may boost brain health!

Spending a few minutes each day reviewing familiar commands can also be grounding for your dog. Reinforcing well-known behaviors (like sitting and staying) can increase healthy brain activity. Plus, it may help your dog remember other things as well! As an extra bonus, those training sessions help to strengthen the bond you have with your dog. This is especially important with cognitive decline.

Additional treatment options

In addition to these environmental modifications, your vet may recommend various supplements, foods, or medications. Supplements like omega-3 fatty acids for dogs and diets with MCTs and Senilife® are available without a prescription. They may help promote brain health and reduce behaviors associated with brain aging. Two prescription diets, Hill's® Prescription Diet® b/d Canine for "brain aging care" and Purina® Neuro Care, and one over-the-counter (OTC) dog food, Purina® Bright Minds, can also be helpful.

As the disease progresses, you may need prescription medications to help with some of the more bothersome symptoms.

- Some dogs may benefit from Selegiline (Anipryl®), a medication designed to help control some of the clinical signs of CCD.

- At first, the OTC supplement melatonin for dogs might help a dog sleep at night. (For safety, always double-check that the melatonin supplement, especially if it is gummies, does not contain xylitol (i.e., birch sugar), which is toxic for dogs.) But when melatonin is no longer effective, your vet may wish to prescribe a sedative to help your dog get appropriate rest.

- Supplements like Anxitane® or Zylkene® can help with mild anxiety. However, when the problem worsens, your dog may need prescription medications like Trazodone or Alprazolam to relax during the day.

What does the progression of CCD look like?

The most troublesome symptoms often start with subtle changes. But as they progress in severity, a dog's quality of life (QOL) can be greatly diminished. For example:

- Getting stuck in the corner once every few days might be bothersome. But when it happens 5 to 10 times a day, the stress can be immeasurable.

- An occasional puddle of urine or a pile of stool might be easy to clean up. But when your dog is soiling the carpet or the bed multiple times a day, it can be frustrating and upsetting to both of you.

- When your dog occasionally paces the house for a few minutes at night, you can both go back to sleep quickly. But when the pacing lasts for hours, and neither of you is able to sleep, you can both have increased stress and decreased overall health.

Not only does your dog's quality of life decline, but you are constantly worrying and running on an empty tank. Your stress level is high. And you don't feel like you have the energy or the patience to give your dog the love and care he or she needs and you wish to provide. As dementia worsens, the precious bond you share with your dog can begin to break…and that is the last thing either of you wants to happen.

How will you know if it's time to euthanize your dog who is suffering from dementia?

Maintaining the human-animal bond should be the most important goal at the end of any dog's life. Dogs adore their human family more than anything else in their lives! So when they are unable to recognize their loved ones, or when the bond has been broken due to mutual stress, anxiety, and lack of sleep, the time has come to set them free from their struggles. Whenever the deep bond between humans and dogs is broken, there is no longer any quality of life. At that point, it may be the kindest decision to make that end-of-life decision and euthanasia.

It is incredibly difficult to consider euthanasia for your canine family member. But it is also incredibly difficult to watch him or her struggle through each day, confused, anxious, and exhausted. Caring for any dog at the end of his or her life is difficult. But perhaps caring for a dog with dementia is the most heart-wrenching.

You wish to be able to comfort your dog, but the old familiar comfort measures no longer work. And when your dog doesn't even recognize you, your presence no longer brings the comfort it once did. You want to give your dog everything he or she needs, but your time and energy are spread thin.

This is very normal, and frustration is an expected response to a very stressful situation. But it often causes caregivers to feel isolated, lonely, and guilty. Giving up sleep, cleaning up after your dog many times every day, bathing him or her often, and having your beloved senior dog lash out at you in frustration and fear can leave you feeling overwhelmed and exhausted.

Your precious old dog needs an abundance of patience, love, and nursing care. That can be difficult to provide, even for the most loving and devoted person.

Euthanasia is a beautiful and selfless decision.

Considering euthanasia can sometimes feel like a selfish decision. "I don't want to euthanize her just because she's hard to care for!" is something that I hear often from distraught pet owners. But every time I hear those words, I hear them coming from a family member who loves their dog deeply and is making a heart-wrenching decision in order to end their dog's struggles. That is the opposite of selfish—it is selfless.

I remind families that they're not choosing euthanasia because their sweet dog is hard to care for. Rather, you realize that your dog's life has grown so difficult that he or she is no longer happy. You don't want to see your dog get any worse. So, you are choosing to provide your dear companion an escape from his or her mental and physical pain. You are focusing on your dog's quality of life above all else, and (while it is incredibly difficult) that is a kind and beautiful decision.

Resources for Navigating the End-of-Life Journey with Your Dog

Saying Goodbye to a beloved pet is never easy, and dementia in dogs adds another layer of complexity to this emotional process. Here are some resources that can offer guidance and support as you make difficult decisions about your dog's well-being:

The logical part of your brain will understand that you are making a loving, merciful decision for your beloved dog. But your heart may never feel ready to let them go—and that is normal.

There will come a time when watching them struggle is harder than setting them free—and that is when you know you are as ready as you will ever be.

Many families want to keep a bit of their dog's fur. They might keep it tucked away in a safe place or make a special ornament to display the fur. Dog parents might like to have ink or clay paw prints—and some people even make artwork out of their dog's painted paw prints!

I often see families make a shadow box with their dog's paw print, a fur clipping, a collar, a photo, or even a special toy. Other families may pick out a special urn for their dog's ashes, create a headstone or a stone marker for the garden, or choose to have a unique piece of glass art made from their dog's ashes. A paw print or a nose print can be memorialized as a necklace, a key chain, or even as a tattoo!

You may choose to have a portrait session with a local photographer during your dog's final months of life. Or you may decide to have a special painting made from one of your favorite snapshots. The possibilities are nearly endless, and finding something that is unique and sentimental can be an important part of your healing process while grieving the loss of your dog after euthanasia.

Letting your dog go is every shade of difficulty.

As a RVT, helping dogs and their families through this difficult time is something I've done hundreds of times. It's not routine by any means, but it is familiar. However, for pet parents, it may be something they are experiencing for the very first time or will only experience a few times during their lifetime. There is nothing familiar or comfortable about it...at all. It's the worst of times.

I can't provide specific medical advice as to determining the right time to let your dog go. I often find myself telling them it's not a black-and-white moment in time—it's a grey zone. But what I can help you with is the fear of the unknown and managing expectations.

While saying goodbye to your dog may be one of the worst days of your life, it can be one of the best days of your dog's life.

First of all, you are making this decision because you know it's time to end your beloved friend's pain and suffering. I hope you can find peace in knowing that the dog is going to be better off. But we can take the "best day" idea one step further.

One of my veterinary colleagues tells his clients to bring chocolate to their dog's euthanasia appointment. In the moments preceding the euthanasia, while the doctor and owners are talking, they feed chocolate pieces to the dog, who thinks heaven has descended on earth.

Lap of Love and Association of Pet Loss and Bereavement are two excellent resources that offer compassionate end-of-life care and euthanasia services currently in the USA.

Before your dog's appointment, speak with your veterinarian about final arrangements such as burial or cremation. Sometimes, discuss the options of burial, affordable communal pet cremation, or private cremation at the beginning of the appointment when heads are clearer. But more often, I discuss these types of decisions with clients well in advance of the painful day. This way, when emotions are raw, the client already knows what they want and doesn't have to give this decision a second thought.

I would encourage you to make a plan in advance of your dog's last day. Also, if cost will play a factor in your decision (because private cremation service is significantly more expensive), call your veterinary hospital to get pricing.

Finding peace and comfort through understanding

Whether you are grieving the loss of your dog or dreading an upcoming decision, I hope somewhere in these words, you are able to find comfort, understanding, and empowerment to reject the guilt you are not meant to carry.

Are you struggling to know when to say goodbye to your dog? Most likely, your canine companion has been by your side through the joys and sorrows of life. He or she has been steadfast in their loyalty and love. You've walked life's path together—both literally and figuratively. Making the decision to let your grey-muzzled companion go may seem unbearable. Euthanasia is not an easy topic to broach, but comfort, hope, and help are here.

This is all any of us can hope for when it comes to pet ownership—to have a beloved animal who becomes like a part of you and lives a good, long life, where each of you makes things better for the other.

But when you are lucky enough to have such a relationship with an old pet, it means you'll also eventually have the burdensome responsibility of deciding when to say goodbye to your dog.

Alleviating suffering: the last gift of love

Unfortunately, pets rarely pass peacefully in their sleep, at least not before enduring an enormous amount of suffering in most cases. Giving them the gift of alleviating that suffering is the last loving, generous act of pet ownership.

Thinking through the goodbye

But how do you know when it is time? One of the hardest factors is that animals often have good days and bad days near the end. On the bad days, especially after several in a row, owners often think it is time to let go. Sometimes, they even make an appointment, only to wake up that morning and find their pet having a great day, which makes them doubt the decision and hold off a bit longer.

This cycle may repeat for weeks or even months and owners are unsure where their responsibility lies. No one wants to give up too soon, nor do they want to wait too long.

Passing peacefully

The reality is that if you really love your pet and you have thought, "It might be time"—it is almost always time. It's just so hard to face that reality. I have had to make the decision for my own senior pets twice in the past two years and it never gets easier.

But it's important to keep in mind that it is a loving gift for them to go peacefully when they are surrounded by people who love them and not alone and scared or in tremendous pain and distress.

Tools to help you know when it is time to say goodbye to your dog

We have already discussed using the Quality of life chart previously but an even easier simple tool that can help is to write on a calendar "good day" or "bad day" and then look back over the last 10-14 days. If the bad days outweigh the good ones, it's time to let your pet go before all of the days are bad.

Another idea is to make a list of your pet's very favorite things to do. When he or she stops doing those two or three things, it is time to say goodbye. Decide in advance that you won't waver, and it will make the decision more objective.

Your dog has given you their very best throughout life, and they deserve to leave with their dignity intact while they can still stand up on their own and they are not incontinent. If you wait until they have completely stopped eating, cannot rise on their own, or are lying in their own waste, you have waited too long.

After more than 40 years working in the veterinary profession, I have talked to countless people who say that, looking back, they wish they hadn't waited so long. But I have never had a single loving pet owner come back and say they regret letting them go too soon.

Again, if you've thought that it might be time, it probably is time.

Your veterinarian can help you through the decision process.

If you are approaching this decision (euthanasia), your veterinarian would be happy to help you through the process and give as much insight as possible into how your pet might be feeling. As veterinarians and RVT's, our job is to advocate for the animals, but we also want to help family members come to a decision that will provide the most peace of mind possible during difficult moments.

- Sometimes, that means making a house call so that pets can pass comfortably in their own homes.

- Sometimes, it means sending home additional medications for hospice care to keep our patients comfortable until other family members can say goodbye.

- Sometimes, it means an owner will sing a song to the pet, take pictures, or select a unique memento to honor the final moments.

- Everyone grieves differently, and there is no judgment from us—only education and compassion.

#1. It is *always* better to be too early rather than too late when making a decision.

More times than I can count over my 40+ years as a RVT, I have found myself sitting on the floor with weeping clients who have come to me to euthanize their failing dog. And they ask, "Are we doing the right thing by letting our dog go today?" (This is particularly true for dog owners caring for elderly dogs.)

While I can't tell them that 2:18 on Thursday afternoon is indeed the "right time," I can reassure them that they are in the right *window of time,* validating their decision to let their dog go with peace and dignity.

My guiding principle in saying goodbye to Peaches was not to eke out every last second of life together but rather to spend every last second of life together *that she could enjoy.*

#2 As much as we all long for it, the odds are slim that our dogs will pass away peacefully in their sleep.

I don't know the actual stats, but I can tell you that very few of my own clients have been given the gift of their faithful canine companion passing gently in the night.

For the vast majority of dog owners, we must be brave and selfless and give our dogs the final gift of a peaceful and painless passing through euthanasia.

After counseling many clients and through my own experience, my heartfelt advice is this: making THE decision will most likely be a part of the journey of life with a dog or cat.

#3 Release some of the pressure by living in the moment and treasuring each day with your dog.

The big, looming question is, "How will I know when it's time to say goodbye to my beloved dog?" I believe, to some extent, that focusing on this question adds additional pressure during an already difficult time. When you recognize that, due to old age or serious illness, your dog is on a downward trend and not recovering, you probably don't have to plan the specific date and hour immediately. Rather, take it one day at a time and consider each additional day as a gift.

"When clients are struggling with THE decision, I advise them to put out two jars. "Every time your dog is having a great day, put a penny in that jar. But every time you think, 'My dog's just not himself, and I'm concerned about his quality of life,' then put a penny in the other jar. Watch the pennies in each jar add up. Pretty soon, it's very obvious."

Keeping a dog health journal is another way to track your dog's good days and bad days. It will help you objectively reflect back on your thoughts and observations over time.

A dog's love lives on

I've read studies claiming that it's harder for people to lose their pets than human loved ones. I'm sure that's not true for us all, but one thing dogs have over humans is this: Dogs embody unconditional love, forgiveness, and joy.

Grieving the Loss of a Dog After Euthanasia (& Finding Peace)

Finding peace in your heart after the goodbye

Grieving the loss of a dog after euthanasia is every shade of difficulty. After listening to a dear friend express the guilt she felt following her dog's euthanasia.

I learned something this week that broke my heart. My friend Jamie has been living with needless guilt for years over the way her dog was euthanized.

Having been a part of many owner present pet euthanasia's, I'm melted each time by the grief, but I've also come to terms with the value of peaceful, gentle euthanasia. However, it never occurred to me that a client might linger in doubt or guilt about the *way* their pet was euthanized.

So, I think it's worth having a hard conversation about grieving the loss of a dog after euthanasia. After Jamie and I talked, she sent me the sweetest message:

"Thank you for the kind words. It puts peace in my heart."

Whether saying goodbye to your dog is a part of your past or your future, I want you to have peace in your heart, too.

Jaimie told me they traveled to the beach. Went to our favorite spot. We spent time with family. And, of course, I spoiled her with her favorite treats.

However, I also knew that words of reassurance, comfort, and truth could help. Here's what Jamie needed to know:

There is no "right" way to perform euthanasia in terms of standard operating procedures. Ultimately, euthanasia is about what is best for the dog. Period.

And after that, it's about determining the preferences of the dog's family. Like most veterinary medicine, helping a dog transition out of this life is more of an art than a science.

The guiding principle for end-of-life care

While there is no "right" protocol for euthanasia, there is a "right" guiding principle. The "right" way to perform euthanasia is to make it physically and emotionally pain-free for the dog. Dog euthanasia is euphemistically referred to as "putting a dog to sleep" for a reason. That's the goal.

Honoring your dog by giving yourself peace

If the guilt of your dog's goodbye lingers in your heart— whether your dog's passing was recent or years ago—I hope you find peace. Ultimately, you were there for your dog in those final moments when he needed you most.

A terminal illness is one where the pet will not be cured or recovered but perhaps can be managed so the pet is comfortable. Treatments at this point are focused on palliative care- helping with pain, nausea, nutrition, hydration, and mobility- but not on curing the pet. Quality of life scales can help the family decide when it is time to let the pet go.

Sometimes, after the discussion, people realize that their pet is enjoying life and they still have time left with their pet. Other times, people realize their pets are suffering more than they were aware of, so they choose the final act of caring. In either case, **the JOURNEYS scale is meant to get you thinking and considering**

the factors that affect your pet's happiness and sense of well-being.

There are no hard and fast rules, although, in general, a higher score is better.

- A score of 80 is a happy, healthy pet!

- A score of 8 is a pet that is suffering. A low score on any of the measures may be a reason to consider euthanasia.

A low score on any one of the variables may be a reason to consider euthanasia if the pet's score cannot be raised. An example of this would be a pet that is still eating and drinking but has pain that cannot be controlled even with pain medications. Another example is a pet that scores 10 socially but has difficulty breathing. We purposely do not give a score to consider euthanasia because every pet, situation, and family is unique. You should consider your pet's individual personality and needs when making a difficult decision.

Eight variables for you to consider:

The JOURNEYS scale addresses eight variables you can use to determine your pet's quality of life. Many people will use the scale daily or weekly to see how their pet is doing and compare the results to see how well the pet has been doing over time.

Different family members can take the scale independently and compare results. These discussions can be helpful in getting a consensus on how to move forward. It is important to use a quality-of-life scale as part of a hospice plan for the pet.

1. Jumping or Mobility
2. Ouch or Pain
3. Uncertainty and Understanding (factors that affect YOU)
4. Respiration or Breathing
5. Neatness or Hygiene
6. Eating and Drinking
7. You
8. Social ability

Chapter 7
Supporting End-of-Life Decisions

The Role of Your Veterinary Team

Saying Goodbye to a beloved pet is never easy. Your veterinary team understands this and wants to help you through this difficult time. They are there to support you as you make important decisions about your pet's end-of-life care.

Here are some ways your veterinary team can be there for you:

1. Understanding Your Pet's Condition: The veterinarian will explain your pet's medical condition and what to expect as the illness progresses. They will also discuss treatment options that can help manage pain and keep your pet comfortable.

2. Quality of Life Discussions: Your veterinary team will talk to you about your pet's quality of life. This means thinking about how your pet feels and their ability to enjoy daily activities. These discussions are important to help you decide what is best for your furry friend.

3. Making Choices: There are no easy answers when it comes to end-of-life decisions. Your veterinarian will present all the options available to you, including hospice care or euthanasia. They will answer your questions and address any concerns you may have to help you make an informed decision.

4. Emotional Support: End-of-life decisions can be very emotional. Your veterinary team will provide compassionate support and understanding throughout this process. They know how much you love your pet, and they will be there for you every step of the way.

Remember, your veterinary team is there to guide you and help you make the best choices for your pet. Don't hesitate to ask questions and express your feelings. They are there to support you through this difficult time.

Understanding Your Pet's Condition: Knowledge is Power

Veterinarians will start by thoroughly explaining your pet's medical condition. This includes their diagnosis, what's causing it, and how it might progress. Studies like the ones published in the Journal of the American Veterinary Medical Association highlight the importance of clear communication. Knowing what to expect helps you make informed choices about your pet's care.

The vet will also discuss treatment options. These might involve medications for pain management, dietary changes, or even specialized therapies. Research by the American Animal Hospital Association emphasizes the role of palliative care in enhancing your pet's comfort during this stage. It's important to understand the potential benefits and limitations of each treatment option before deciding which path to take.

Quality of Life: It's All About Your Pet

Beyond the medical details, vets will also focus on your pet's quality of life. This isn't just about physical health but also about their emotional well-being and ability to enjoy daily activities. Can your pet still eat, play, and interact with you? Are they experiencing pain or discomfort that outweighs any happy moments?

Studies by the Companion Animal Euthanasia Research Project have shown that owners often struggle with this concept. Vets can help by providing quality-of-life assessment tools and discussing how your pet's condition might affect their daily happiness.

Your Veterinary Team: Your Source of Strength

Your veterinarian is more than just a doctor for your pet; they're a trusted advisor during this challenging time. Their team, including Registered Veterinary Technicians and support staff, will provide valuable guidance and emotional support.

Palliative care focuses on managing your pet's symptoms and pain rather than curing the underlying disease. It might include:

- Medication adjustments for pain relief, nausea, or anxiety

- Dietary modifications for easier digestion and better nutrition
- Supportive therapies like massage or acupuncture (depending on your pet's condition)

Palliative care doesn't aim to extend life but rather to improve its quality for as long as possible. While costs vary depending on medications and therapies used, it's generally less expensive than aggressive treatment options. The effectiveness lies in your pet's improved comfort and ability to enjoy life's little pleasures.

Hospice Care

When treatment options can no longer significantly improve your pet's quality of life, hospice care offers a compassionate approach to their final days.

Similar to human hospice care, this focuses on comfort and symptom management in a familiar environment, often your own home. Hospice care typically involves:

- Pain medication and other supportive medications
- Dietary guidance and feeding assistance, if needed
- Regular visits from a veterinarian or hospice team member
- Emotional support for both you and your pet

Studies like those published by the AAHA show that hospice care can significantly improve pet owners' confidence and reduce anxiety during this sensitive time.

The cost of hospice care can vary depending on the frequency of visits and medications needed. Many veterinary practices have partnered with hospice care providers, offering a comprehensive and affordable package.

Effectiveness? Hospice care doesn't extend life, but it allows your pet to spend their remaining time comfortably and surrounded by loved ones. This can be an invaluable gift for both your pet and yourself.

Euthanasia

Euthanasia, also known as putting your pet to sleep, is a humane way to end their suffering when treatment options are no longer effective or their quality of life is severely compromised. Research by the American College of Veterinary Internal Medicine emphasizes the importance of compassionate euthanasia practices, minimizing stress for both pets and owners.

The process typically involves a painless injection that sends your pet peacefully to sleep. You can choose to be present during the procedure, and many veterinary clinics offer private rooms for this sensitive moment.

Here are some signs that euthanasia might be the kindest option:

- Uncontrollable pain despite medication
- Inability to eat, drink, or use the bathroom without assistance
- Significant loss of mobility or ability to enjoy favorite activities
- Difficulty breathing or other signs of distress

The cost of euthanasia can vary depending on the clinic and location.

The effectiveness of euthanasia lies in ending your pet's suffering and allowing it to pass peacefully.

Saying a Final Farewell: Aftercare Options

After saying Goodbye, you may need to make decisions about your pet's remains.

Emotional Support: You're Not Alone

End-of-life decisions can be incredibly emotional. Veterinarians and their staff understand that. They'll provide a safe space for you to express your feelings, ask questions, and voice your concerns. Don't hesitate to talk about your worries, fears, or even guilt. Your vet can help validate your emotions and offer support throughout this process.

Many veterinary practices offer resources like grief counseling or support groups for pet owners. Additionally, organizations like the Lap of Love or the Association for Pet Loss and Bereavement offer resources and support for pet owners dealing with loss.

Remember: It's About Your Pet's Well-Being

Ultimately, the decision you make should be based on what's best for your pet. Think about what would bring them comfort and alleviate their suffering. There's no right or wrong answer. Trust your gut, rely on your veterinarian's expertise, and know that you're not alone in this difficult time.

Your veterinary team is there to guide you through every step of the process, from understanding your pet's condition to navigating treatment options and emotional support. Don't hesitate to reach out and ask for help.

Chapter 8

Finding Support

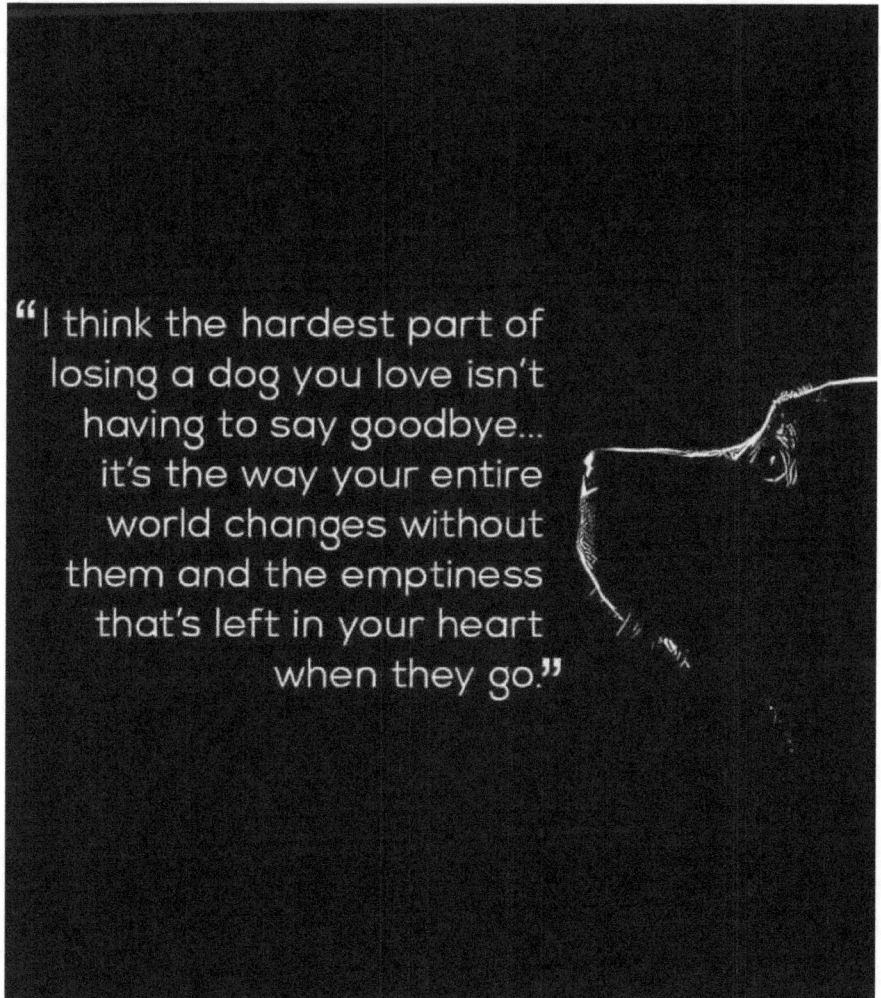

"I think the hardest part of losing a dog you love isn't having to say goodbye... it's the way your entire world changes without them and the emptiness that's left in your heart when they go."

Coping with the Loss: Support for the Owner Now That the Pet is Gone

The unconditional love and companionship a pet offers create a profound bond. When that pet passes away, the grief can be overwhelming. It's important to remember that the depth of your sorrow reflects the depth of the love you shared. There is no right or wrong way to grieve, and the journey through pet loss is unique to each individual.

The article Coping with the grief of pet loss explores resources and support systems available to help you navigate the emotional rollercoaster following the loss of your beloved pet. We'll focus on two key areas: pet loss support groups and pet loss counselors.

Pet Loss Support Groups: Sharing the Burden

Pet loss support groups provide a safe and compassionate space for grieving pet owners to connect with others who understand the unique pain of losing a furry (or feathered or scaled) friend. Sharing your experiences and emotions with those who have walked a similar path can be incredibly validating and comforting. Here's what you can expect from a pet loss support group:

- **Understanding and Empathy:** Unlike some friends or family who might not fully grasp the depth of your grief, support group members have experienced a similar loss. They can listen without judgment and offer empathy born from shared experience.

- **Sharing Stories and Memories:** Being able to openly reminisce about your pet and celebrate their life can be a powerful part of the healing process. Support groups provide a platform to share stories and photos, keeping your pet's memory alive.

- **Learning Coping Mechanisms:** Hearing how others have coped with their loss can provide valuable tools and strategies for managing your own grief. You might learn relaxation techniques, journaling exercises, or ways to create memorials for your pet.

- **Reduced Isolation:** The intense emotions associated with pet loss can make you feel isolated. Support groups help combat this by connecting you with a community of understanding individuals.

Finding a Pet Loss Support Group:

Many local animal shelters, veterinary clinics, and pet stores host pet loss support groups. Online platforms can also be a great resource - look for groups on social media platforms or dedicated pet loss websites.

Here are some tips for finding a support group that's right for you:

- **Consider the format:** Choose an in-person group if you crave face-to-face interaction, or opt for online groups if the virtual connection is more comfortable.

- **Size and Structure:** Decide if you prefer a small, intimate group or a larger one offering diverse perspectives. Some groups are facilitated by a professional counselor, while others are more informal peer-support groups.

- **Focus and Approach:** Some groups may cater to specific types of loss, such as sudden death or euthanasia. Others may implement specific grief management techniques.

NO MATTER HOW LONG WE HAVE WITH THEM, IT'S NEVER LONG ENOUGH

Pet Loss Counselors: Professional Guidance on the Grieving Path

Sometimes, the weight of grief may feel overwhelming, and you might need additional support beyond a support group. Pet loss counselors are mental health professionals specializing in helping individuals and families cope with the loss of a pet. They can provide:

- **Individualized Support:** Counselors tailor their approach to your unique needs and grief experience. They create a safe space for you to express your emotions openly and explore coping mechanisms that work best for you.

- **Grief Management Techniques:** Counselors can teach you techniques such as cognitive behavioral therapy (CBT) or mindfulness to manage strong emotions and navigate the stages of grief.

- **Dealing with Complexities:** Pet loss can be compounded by other factors like depression or anxiety. Counselors can help you address these underlying issues alongside your pet-related grief.

Finding a Pet Loss Counselor:

Many therapists specialize in animal bereavement. You can start your search by asking your veterinarian for a referral or checking online directories of mental health professionals. When choosing a counselor, consider:

- **Credentials and Experience:** Look for a licensed therapist with experience in pet loss counseling.

- **Therapeutic Approach:** Some therapists utilize specific techniques like CBT, while others offer more general support.

- **Personality Fit:** Finding a counselor you feel comfortable and safe with is crucial. Don't hesitate to ask for a free consultation to see if you establish a good rapport.

Additional Resources:

There are many resources available online and in your community to help you through pet loss. Here are some helpful options:

- **The Association for Pet Loss and Bereavement (APLB):** APLB offers a wealth of resources, including a toll-free helpline, chat rooms, and online forums: https://www.aplb.org/.

- **Lap of Love:** This organization provides pet loss support, including virtual support groups and articles on coping with pet loss https://petloss.lapoflove.com/.

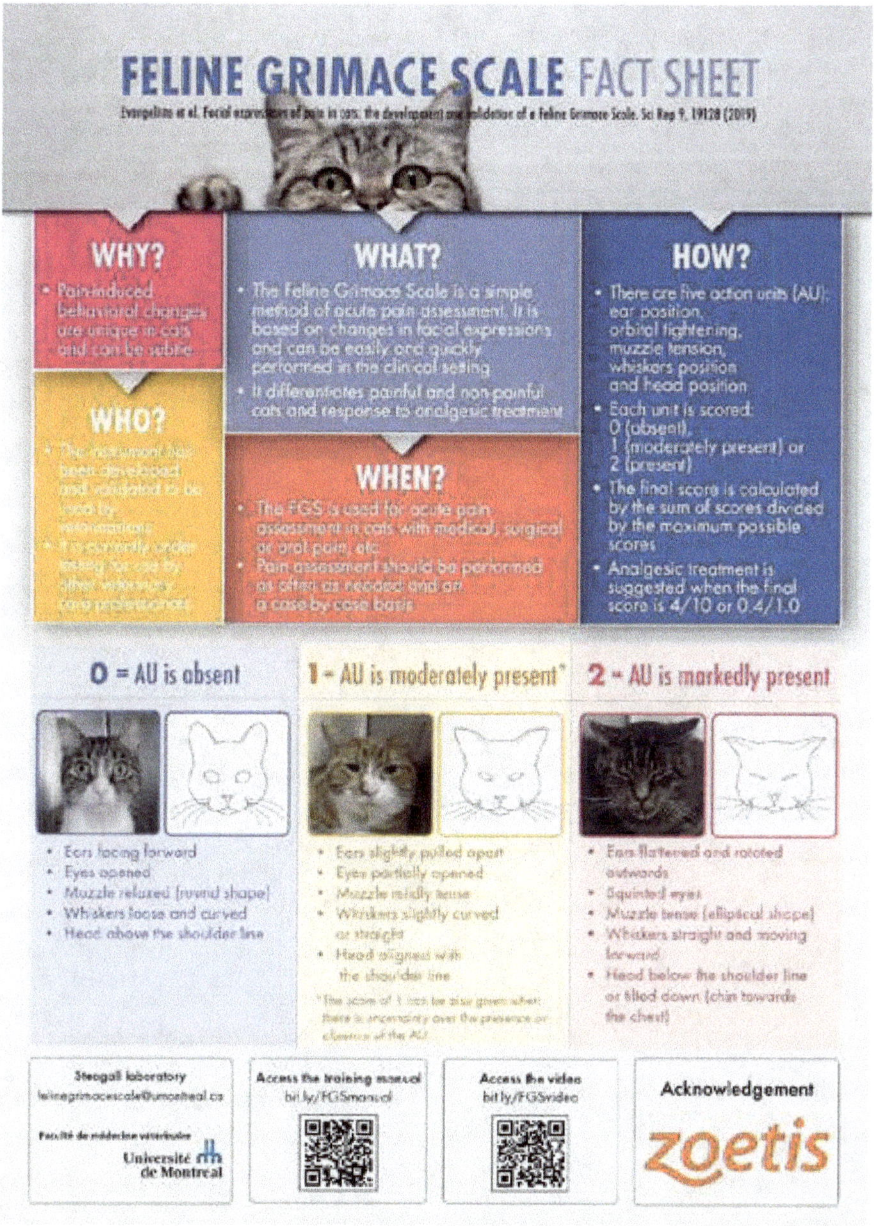
FELINE GRIMACE SCALE FACT SHEET
WHY?
• Pain-induced behavioral changes are unique in cats and can be subtle
WHAT?
• The Feline Grimace Scale is a simple method of acute pain assessment. It is based on changes in facial expressions and can be easily and quickly performed in the clinical setting
• It differentiates painful and non-painful cats and response to analgesic treatment
HOW?
• There are five action units (AU): ear position, orbital tightening, muzzle tension, whiskers position and head position
• Each unit is scored: 0 (absent), 1 (moderately present) or 2 (present)
• The final score is calculated by the sum of scores divided by the maximum possible scores
• Analgesic treatment is suggested when the final score is 4/10 or 0.4/1.0
WHO?
WHEN?
• The FGS is used for acute pain assessment in cats with medical, surgical or oral pain, etc
• Pain assessment should be performed as often as needed and on a case by case basis
0 = AU is absent
• Ears facing forward
• Eyes opened
• Muzzle relaxed (round shape)
• Whiskers loose and curved
• Head above the shoulder line
1 = AU is moderately present*
• Ears slightly pulled apart
• Eyes partially opened
• Muzzle mildly tense
• Whiskers slightly curved or straight
• Head aligned with the shoulder line
2 = AU is markedly present
• Ears flattened and rotated outwards
• Squinted eyes
• Muzzle tense (elliptical shape)
• Whiskers straight and moving forward
• Head below the shoulder line or tilted down (chin towards the chest)
Steagall laboratory
Université de Montréal
Access the training manual
bit.ly/FGSmanual
Access the video
bit.ly/FGSvideo
Acknowledgement
zoetis

BEAP Pain Scale for Cats

PetHospice.com

Many signs of chronic pain are non-specific. Make sure to see your vet to rule out other disease as a cause of these signs.

0
No Pain

- [ ] **B:** Breathing normally
- [ ] **E:** Eyes bright and alert
- [ ] **A:** Walks normally and remains agile
- [ ] **A:** Engages in play and all normal activities
- [ ] **A:** Eating and drinking normally
- [ ] **A:** Happy and content; interested in surroundings; playful behavior; seeks attention
- [ ] **P:** Comfortable at rest and during play; perky ears; upright, alert tail; whiskers relaxed
- [ ] **P:** Enjoys being touched, petted and brushed; no body tension present

1-2
Mild Pain

Speak to your vet during your next appointment

- [ ] **B:** Breathing normally
- [ ] **E:** Eyes bright and alert
- [ ] **A:** Slightly more hesitant to jump onto very high places such as counter tops but still able to easily jump onto couch or bed
- [ ] **A:** May show only subtle change in normal activity and behaviors
- [ ] **A:** Eating and drinking normally
- [ ] **A:** Will often still remain happy and interested in surroundings
- [ ] **P:** May be down just a little more; ears up; whiskers generally appear relaxed
- [ ] **P:** Enjoys being touched, petted and brushed; no body tension present

3-4
Moderate Pain

See your vet to assess pain

- [ ] **B:** Breathing generally normal but may be at slightly increased rate
- [ ] **E:** Eyes may be slightly more dull in appearance; eyes may be held partially closed
- [ ] **A:** Hesitant to jump to higher places; may also not jump onto lower places, such as couch or bed
- [ ] **A:** Not eager to interact but still in tune with surroundings; changes in normal routine; may hide; decreased grooming
- [ ] **A:** Appetite more finicky, such as wanting only treats or "junk" food such as canned food
- [ ] **A:** Generally more subdued and quiet
- [ ] **P:** Difficulty posturing to eliminate or cover waste; subtle changes in posture; tail held low and ears more flattened, whiskers slightly down
- [ ] **P:** Does not mind touch except on painful area; turns head to look where touched; mild body tension

5-6
Moderate to Severe Pain

CONCERNING! See your vet

- [ ] **B:** Breathing rate and effort may be increased
- [ ] **E:** Dull eyes; eyes may remain partially or fully closed; pupils may be more dilated
- [ ] **A:** Moves more slowly or gingerly; no longer jumps up onto couch or bed; difficulty on stairs
- [ ] **A:** Withdraws from family and other pets; seeks solitude; decreased grooming; may excessively lick painful area; may have "accidents" outside the litter box
- [ ] **A:** Will frequently lose appetite
- [ ] **A:** Very subdued and quiet; increased facial tension; decreased enjoyment of being brushed
- [ ] **P:** "Meatloaf" position; whiskers move forward slightly from face; rough or fluffed up fur; difficulty posturing to eliminate or cover waste fully
- [ ] **P:** Pulls away painful area or tries to escape; moderate body tension when being touched

7-8
Severe Pain

VERY CONCERNING! See your vet

- [ ] **B:** Faster breathing rate with more noticeable effort
- [ ] **E:** Dull eyes; generally remain partially or fully closed; may have distressed look; pupils dilated
- [ ] **A:** Unlikely to move if left alone
- [ ] **A:** Avoids all interaction; will "go off" and hide, often in new places; stops grooming; frequently licks or chews at painful area, sometimes to the point of fur loss
- [ ] **A:** Loss of appetite; may not want to drink
- [ ] **A:** Reclusive; agitated; potentially aggressive; tail flicking; may be growling or hissing
- [ ] **P:** Tail held close, ears flattened or pinned back, whiskers move forward and tend to bunch; "grimace face"; flattened posture
- [ ] **P:** Significant body tension when painful area touched; may growl or hiss in pain; guards painful area by pulling away or trying to escape

9-10
Worst Pain Possible

EMERGENCY! See your vet

- [ ] **B:** Increased breathing rate and effort; may have periods of open-mouthed breathing or panting
- [ ] **E:** Dull closed eyes; eyes may also widen with a look of panic; pupils dilated
- [ ] **A:** Unable or unwilling to walk
- [ ] **A:** Difficulty in being distracted from pain, even with gentle touch or soothing voice; may bite or chew painful area; may eliminate where lying
- [ ] **A:** No interest in food or water
- [ ] **A:** Extremely depressed or minimally responsive ("flat out"); quiet, growling or hissing; distressed
- [ ] **P:** Lying on side; tail may appear "fluffed"
- [ ] **P:** Rigid body tension when touched; will not tolerate touch of painful area; hissing when other areas that are not painful are touched

Specific behaviors or physical changes I see:

Breathing: _____
Eyes: _____
Ambulation: _____
Activity: _____
Appetite: _____
Attitude: _____
Posture: _____
Palpation: _____

© 2018
Shea Cox

BEAP Pain Scale for Dogs

PetHospice.com

Many signs of chronic pain are non-specific. Make sure to see your vet to rule out other disease as a cause of these signs.

0
No
Pain

- B: Breathing normally
- E: Eyes bright and alert
- A: Walks normally on all four legs; no lameness present
- A: Engages in play and all normal activities
- A: Eating and drinking normally
- A: Happy, interested in surroundings and playing; seeks attention
- P: Comfortable at rest and during play; perky ears and wagging tail
- P: Enjoys being touched and petted; no body tension present

1-2
Mild
Pain

Speak to your vet during a visit or appointment

- B: Breathing normally
- E: Eyes bright and alert
- A: Walks normally; may exhibit very subtle lameness when walking
- A: May show first signs of being just a little more slow to lie down or rise up (subtle)
- A: Eating and drinking normally
- A: Happy and engaged; may seem a little more subdued with some "off" moments interspersed with normal behaviors
- P: May show occasional shifting of position; tail may be down just a little more, ears slightly flatter
- P: Enjoys being touched and petted; no body tension present

3-4
Moderate
Pain

See your vet as soon as possible

- B: May pant intermittently
- E: Eyes slightly more dull in appearance; can have a slightly furrowed brow
- A: Noticeably slower to lie down or rise up; may exhibit lameness when walking
- A: May be slightly unsettled and more restless; difficulty getting comfortable; shifting weight
- A: Appetite more finicky, such as wanting only treats or "people" food
- A: Subdued; engages less or does not initiate play
- P: Difficulty squatting or lifting leg to urinate; subtle changes in posture; tail more tucked and ears more flattened
- P: Does not mind touch except on painful area; turns head to look where touched; mild body tension

5-6
Moderate
to Severe
Pain

CONCERNING!
See your vet

- B: Panting often noted; possibly with an increased breathing effort
- E: Dull eyes, worried look
- A: Very slow to rise up and lie down; hesitation with movement; difficulty on stairs; reluctant to come when called; more obvious lameness
- A: Not eager to interact but may be in tune with surroundings; obvious lameness when walking; may lick painful area
- A: Will frequently lose appetite
- A: Anxious, unsettled or restless; unable to settle or sleep well
- P: Abnormal weight distribution when standing; difficulty posturing to eliminate; arched back, tucked belly, head hanging low; tucked tail; frequently shifts positions; ears more flattened
- P: Pulls away painful area when touched; moderate body tension when being touched

7-8
Severe
Pain

VERY
CONCERNING!
See your vet

- B: Faster breathing rate with more noticeable effort; frequent panting episodes common
- E: Dull eyes, may also have distressed look
- A: Obvious difficulty rising up or lying down; will not bear weight on affected leg; avoids stairs; obvious lameness
- A: Avoids interaction with family or environment; will often "go off" or hide; may frequently lick painful areas
- A: Loss of appetite; may not want to drink
- A: Agitated, fearful, worried, reclusive, potentially aggressive
- P: Tail tucked, ears flattened or pinned back; abnormal posture when standing; more hesitant to move or stand
- P: Significant body tension when painful area touched; may vocalize in pain; guards painful area by pulling away or changing position

9-10
Worst
Pain
Possible

EMERGENCY!
See your vet

- B: Panting, increased breathing rate and effort
- E: Dull eyes, may have panicked look
- A: May refuse to get up, may not be able to or willing to take more than a few steps; will not bear weight on painful limb
- A: Difficulty in being distracted from pain, even with gentle touch or soothing voice
- A: No interest in food or water
- A: Extremely depressed or minimally responsive ("flat out"); may vocalize in pain; in distress at rest
- P: Prefers lying position or being on side; flat or pinned ears; may prefer to be very tucked up or stretched out
- P: Severe body tension when touched; will not tolerate touch of painful area; becomes fearful when other areas that are not painful are touched

Specific behaviors or physical changes I see:

Breathing: _____
Eyes: _____
Ambulation: _____
Activity: _____
Appetite: _____
Attitude: _____
Posture: _____
Palpation: _____

© 2014
Shea Cox

PET QUALITY OF LIFE SCALE AND DAILY DIARY

Directions: Use the key factors of quality of life below to help assess your pet's condition. Use the Daily Diary to keep track of your pet's progress. Fill in the appropriate number for each category and then add the numbers from each category for that day. The maximum score is 12 and you can determine your own scale. You can even add categories that pertain to your pet's particular situation. For example, Respiratory Rate if your pet suffers from heart failure or lung cancer. You can give half or quarter points if appropriate.

MOBILITY

2 **Good Mobility** - No difficulty getting around, enjoys walks and going outside

1 **Poor Mobility** - Difficulty getting up, hard to get in position to eliminate, short walks only

0 **Bare Minimum Mobility** - Needs assistance, pain medication/ anti-inflammatory medication, cannot rise

NUTRITION

2 **Good Appetite**

1 **Poor Appetite** - Hand feeding, needs enticing

0 **No Appetite**

HYDRATION

2 **Adequate Intake**

1 **Poor Intake** (or increased in some pets with particular diseases)

0 **No Intake** (not drinking)

INTERACTION/ATTITUDE

2 **Interacts Normally** with family and other pets

1 **Some Interaction** with family and other pets

0 **Hides** in the closet or under the bed

ELIMINATION

2 **Normal** urination and/or defecation

1 **Reduced/Irregular** urination and/or defecation

0 **None**

FAVORITE THINGS

2 **Normal** favorite activities, toddles, etc

1 **Decrease** in doing their favorite things

0 **No Interest** in their favorite things

EXAMPLE SCALE IS AS FOLLOWS

12-9   Everything is okay

8-8   Requires intervention

< or = 5   Consider humane tranquilization and euthanasia

DAILY DIARY

Date	Mobility	Nutrition	Hydration	Interaction/ Attitude	Elimination	Favorite Things	Total & Daily Notes

Thank you to Lap of Love for consent
www.lapoflove.com

Powered By
GATEWAY

Remember, Healing Takes Time:

Everyone grieves differently. Be patient with yourself and allow yourself to feel the full range of emotions associated with your loss. There is no set timeline for healing. Some days will be harder than others, and that's okay.

Signs & Symptoms of Grief: Normal Effects of Bereavement

Let's just recap what we have already discussed in this book and bring the conversation full circle.

Grief, the emotional response to loss, can manifest in surprising ways. While the experience may feel overwhelming and even bizarre at times, it's important to know that most of these symptoms are perfectly normal parts of the grieving process.

The physical, emotional, social, and spiritual effects of bereavement, along with some unusual experiences you might encounter. We'll also discuss when it's time to seek professional help.

Exhaustion: The Physical Toll of Grief

Grief takes a significant physical toll. You might experience:

- **Fatigue:** The emotional work of grieving is draining. Fatigue is normal and usually improves over time.

- **Sleep Disruption:** Insomnia, excessive sleep, or disturbing dreams are common. Avoid relying on medication for sleep. Opt for natural remedies like Valerian Root or melatonin in moderation.

- **Digestive Issues:** Loss of appetite, overeating, nausea, and stomach upset are all possible. Your digestive system will settle down as you heal.

- **Physical Anxiety:** Headaches, shortness of breath, chest pressure, and tightness in the throat can occur. If mild and improving, they're likely related to grief. However, seek immediate medical attention for severe chest pain and shortness of breath with nausea or sweating, as these could be signs of a heart attack.

Fears and Somatic Symptoms:

If your beloved pet died from illness, it's natural to fear getting sick yourself. You might even experience similar physical symptoms out of worry. If any physical effects persist or worsen, consult a doctor to rule out any underlying medical conditions.

Emotional Rollercoaster: The Ups and Downs of Grief

Grief is a whirlwind of emotions. Don't be surprised by the constant shifts – it's all part of the process. As long as your feelings are evolving, you're on the right track.

Numbness: Initially, you might experience shock, numbness, or disbelief. This is a natural defense mechanism to protect you from the overwhelming pain. However, avoiding the pain won't make it disappear – processing it is crucial for healing.

Sadness and Yearning: Profound sadness and missing the physical presence of your pet are inevitable. Allow yourself to cry – it's a healthy release.

Relief and Guilt: Even in difficult relationships, a sense of relief may accompany death. This feeling can be followed by guilt. You might have "survivor's guilt" or regrets about things left unsaid. Remember, these are common emotions – you're not alone.

Anxiety, Fear, and the Mental Fog of Grief

Grief can trigger a wave of anxiety and fear. You might feel helpless, panicked, or even embarrassed at times. These are all normal responses to a significant loss. Remember, the intensity of these emotions will lessen as you heal.

Mental Challenges: Grief can cloud your thinking. Trouble concentrating, finishing tasks, forgetting things, and difficulty making decisions are all common. It's wise to avoid major life decisions during this period.

Anger: A Universal Emotion

Anger is a powerful and natural reaction to loss. You might be angry at your pet for leaving, the situation that caused the death, the medical professionals, or even God. Find healthy ways to express this anger: scream into a pillow, talk to a friend, write in a journal, or create art that reflects your emotions. Don't force yourself to forgive – acknowledge and process your anger before letting it go.

Navigating Shifting Social Circles After a Loss

Grief can significantly impact your social life. Here's what you might experience:

Shifting Support: Immediately following a loss, you'll likely receive an abundance of support from friends and family. This may wane with time – flowers stop arriving, and people resume their routines. This can leave you feeling abandoned at a time when you need support the most.

Uncomfortable Friendships: Some friends may find it difficult to cope with your grief and unintentionally withdraw. They might not know what to say or how to help, leading them to avoid you altogether.

Social Withdrawal: You might withdraw from social activities as a way to process your emotions. Feeling isolated or disinterested in your usual hobbies is common.

Irritability and Suspicion: Grief can manifest as irritability or suspicion towards others. This can be due to feeling misunderstood and struggling with their lack of empathy.

The Road Ahead:

Gradually, your social life will adapt as you heal. While some friendships might change permanently, others will strengthen. Remember, this is a normal part of the grieving process.

Spiritual Reassessment: Questioning Faith After Loss

Grief can trigger a spiritual crisis. You might question your faith, feel angry at a higher power, or grapple with the meaning of life after loss. Why did this happen? Was it part of a plan?

There are no easy answers here. Spirituality is a personal journey. Religious rituals and prayer might offer solace during this time. Allow yourself to explore your doubts and questions – they'll likely evolve as you heal.

Weird & Wonderful: Unusual Experiences During Grief

You might think you've moved past the initial stages of grief, only to be surprised by an unexpected wave of emotion. Don't be alarmed by these experiences – they're perfectly normal.

Here are some common yet unusual occurrences during grief:

- **Sensory Experiences:** Feeling like you see, hear, smell, or sense the presence of your pet. These are vivid memories, not ghosts.

- **Memory Lapses:** Struggling to recall specific details about your beloved pet – this is temporary, and a more balanced memory will return.

- **Preoccupation and Obsession:** Having frequent thoughts about your loved one is natural.

- **Treasuring Mementos:** Holding onto belongings that represent your beloved pet is a way to keep their memory alive.

- **Vivid Dreams:** Experiencing vivid and even disturbing dreams about your loved one is common.

Remember, these experiences are a normal part of the grieving process. They may feel strange, but they don't indicate a mental breakdown.

When to Seek Professional Help: Navigating Complicated Grief

While most people navigate grief on their own, some experience a more complex form known as complicated grief. This chapter explores the warning signs that indicate you might benefit from professional support.

The Flow of Grief:

Remember, grief is a journey, not a destination. It's characterized by a constant shift in emotions. Feeling exhausted but able to process your feelings is a sign you're on the right track.

Red Flags: When Grief Becomes Stagnant

Grief becomes complicated when it stagnates. If you feel stuck in a constant state of intense sadness, unable to function in daily life, or have a sense of unfinished business with your loved one, it's time to seek help.

Exaggerated Grief:

In rare cases, grief becomes overwhelming and disabling. This may manifest as psychotic behavior, antisocial tendencies, or suicidal thoughts. If you experience these symptoms, reaching out to a therapist specializing in grief is crucial.

Warning Signs to Heed:

- **Suicidal Thoughts:** It's common to have fleeting thoughts of wanting to join your loved one. However, persistent suicidal thoughts or planning an act of self-harm require immediate professional help. Don't hesitate to talk to someone and seek support.

- **High Anxiety:** While some anxiety is normal during grief, if you feel overwhelmed by fear or experience frequent panic attacks, consider seeking help from a counselor.

- **Depression:** Grief shares some characteristics with depression, but they are distinct. Grief is a natural response to loss, while depression is a clinical disorder with a physiological cause.

Here's a key difference:

- **Grief:** A normal emotional response, not a mental illness. Sadness is expected, and there's no need for medication. It needs time to run its course.

- **Depression:** A clinical disorder requiring treatment, often through medication and sometimes psychotherapy.

Avoiding Shortcuts:

Don't resort to anti-anxiety medication or excessive alcohol to cope with grief. These are temporary solutions with potentially harmful consequences. Remember, the healing process takes time and dedication.

Normal Grief vs. Clinical Depression: Understanding the Differences

Grief and depression can share similar symptoms, making it difficult to distinguish between the two. Here's a breakdown to help you understand the key differences:

Normal Grief:

- **Self-Esteem:** While sadness is present, self-esteem remains intact. Grief feels like a natural and expected response.

- **Emotions:** A rollercoaster of emotions is normal, including sadness, anger, guilt, and yearning. These emotions tend to fluctuate and gradually lessen over time.

- **Focus:** The focus might be on the lost loved one and memories, but there's still an ability to engage in other aspects of life.

- **Duration:** The intensity of grief lessens over time, even though sadness may linger. There's a gradual return to a sense of normalcy.

- **Treatment:** Support groups, grief counseling, and self-care practices can be helpful in navigating grief. Medication is typically not required.

Clinical Depression:

- **Self-Esteem:** A persistent negative view of oneself is a hallmark symptom. Feelings of worthlessness and hopelessness are common.

- **Emotions:** Sadness is pervasive and unrelenting. There's a lack of motivation and a diminished ability to experience joy.

- **Focus:** Daily activities become difficult, and there's a withdrawal from social interaction and hobbies.

- **Duration:** Symptoms persist for weeks or even months without improvement.

- **Treatment:** Medication, combined with psychotherapy, is often the most effective treatment for depression.

A Helpful Analogy:

As the quote suggests, grief makes the world seem empty, while depression makes the person themselves feel empty.

Dogs come
into our lives
to teach us about
love... they depart to
teach us about loss. a
new dog never replaces an old dog.
it merely expands the heart.
If you have loved many
dogs, your heart
is very
big.

Important Note:

If you're unsure whether you're experiencing normal grief or clinical depression, it's crucial to seek professional help. A doctor or therapist can provide a diagnosis and recommend the most appropriate treatment plan.

Story of Trixie, Tucker, and Sunny

Remember, if you have other pets at home, you need to watch how they react emotionally after your pet has died and is no longer part of the family. This might seem strange, so let me share a real-life example to help you understand what I mean.

Trixie was a 10-year-old Jack Russell Terrier I had kept from a litter of mine. When she was 6 years old, she developed swelling in the joints of both front legs, making it painful for her to walk at times. Her veterinarian diagnosed her with immune arthritis, which is similar to rheumatoid arthritis in humans. This condition doesn't go away but can be managed with steroids, pain medications, supplements, and a diet change.

The biggest challenge with Trixie was that she always wanted to be included in everything. Even with her mobility issues, it was hard to keep her confined and calm. Despite the pain medications, she still wanted to be part of all the activities, making it difficult to restrict her movements.

I made a promise to Trixie that when her pain became unmanageable, I would let her go peacefully to stop her suffering. We managed to keep her comfortable and relatively pain-free for four years. She had good days and bad days, and I used a calendar to track her quality of life.

Just before Thanksgiving 2020, in the middle of the afternoon, she went outside as usual, but her hind legs gave out, and she couldn't walk anymore. The decision was made for me, and I knew it was time to fulfill my promise to her.

I called the vet clinic to let them know we were on our way and that I had decided on owner-present euthanasia. They were prepared for us when we arrived, ensuring Trixie's final moments were peaceful and surrounded by love.

The entire process was smooth and special as I said goodbye to Trixie. She understood completely, and her tail wagged, letting me know she was also saying goodbye.

When I arrived back home, I was greeted by Trixie's companion, Tucker, our 4-year-old Jack Russell Terrier. He was excited to see us but looked lost because Trixie wasn't with us. For several days, he moped around the house, stayed very quiet, didn't eat much, and even started following our cats around.

It was clear to me that Tucker was mourning the loss of his companion. Even though I wasn't ready to add a new puppy to our household, I felt I had no choice.

It has been three months since Trixie passed, and I started searching for a new companion for Tucker. The biggest hurdle was that it was 2020, the COVID pandemic had just started, and we were in lockdown. None of my Jack Russell Terrier breeder friends had puppies. We even considered adopting from the SPCA, but there were no dogs available there either.

Another month went by, and we were on the waitlist with two breeders for a puppy, which would take another six months. I decided that if I had to wait, I wanted another tan and white broken-coated female Jack Russell Terrier, just like my first JRT, Peaches.

As I mentioned at the beginning of this book, I firmly believe that our pets choose us and come into our lives when we need them the most. And that is exactly what happened next. We were contacted by a breeder friend who happened to have a female JRT— tan and white with a broken coat. She was born in February 2021 and will be available in April 2021.

I went to meet this puppy, fell in love with her, and brought her home that very day.

When I came home with Little Miss Sunshine, aka Sunny, in the crate and put her on the floor for Tucker to meet, it was love at first sight for him. He instantly became his old self, full of life. It was truly remarkable to witness the instant change in his demeanor, validating my decision to add a new puppy so soon. After all, it had only been six months since Trixie had passed.

Sunny brought joy back into our home, not just for Tucker but for all of us. Her playful energy and sweet nature helped heal our hearts and made us feel complete again.

So please pay attention to the other pets you may have in your home as they may be experiencing grief of their own and will need some attention and help to get them through it too.

Maybe adding another pet is the right choice for you, but maybe it is not. The answer to this can only be decided by you and only you. It can also be a family decision, and when the time is right you will know, and that special new family member will show up for you when you least expect it to happen.

I hope you find what you are looking for here within the pages of my book. Remember you are not alone and life will get better over time once you have found your way thought the stages of grief and sadness to the other side where cherished memories live along with happiness.

Sincerely,

Nancy MacFarlane RVT

If you would like to share your personal journey of grief with me, feel free to email me - comfortafterpetloss@gmail.com